SCHINDLER

Schindler

DAVID GEBHARD

Preface by

HENRY-RUSSELL HITCHCOCK

A STUDIO BOOK

THE VIKING PRESS · NEW YORK

1   *frontispiece* Rudolph M. Schindler about 1941

Published in 1972 in a hardbound and paperbound edition by
The Viking Press, Inc.
625 Madison Avenue, New York 10022

SBN 670–62063–7 (hardbound)
SBN 670–02022–2 (paperbound)

Library of Congress catalog card number: 71–172899

Printed in Great Britain by Jarrold and Sons Ltd, Norwich

Contents

Acknowledgments

Our present awareness of Schindler is due entirely to the efforts of Esther McCoy, who not only knew and worked as a draughtsman for the architect, but has continued to write about his work for almost a quarter of a century. The chapter on Schindler in her volume, *Five California Architects* (1960), was for most non-Californians their first introduction to this architect. Others who have been of tremendous help are Pauline Schindler, Mark and Mary Schindler, Robin Middleton, Allan Temko, Reyner Banham, John Reed, Robert Winter, Marvin Rand and Julius Shulman. My wife Patricia not only typed the manuscript, but, as always, forced me to rethink a number of important problems.

All illustrations except those listed below are due to The Art Galleries of the University of California, Santa Barbara, who also possess Schindler's original sketches, working drawings, specifications, correspondence, photographs, clippings and models.
The Architectural Forum (January 1940) 125, (April 1940) 109; Viroque Baker 50, 68; J. T. Beals 83, 84, 85; *California Arts and Architecture* (January 1930) 78, (January 1935) 108; Robert C. Cleveland 152, 153; Crescent Photo Shop, Avalon, Calif. 74; Alice Erving 30; A. F. Fog 89; David Gebhard 76, 110; Robert A. Lodder 158; Los Angeles County Museum of Natural History, History Division 2; Lotte Nossaman 154, 155; Ernest M. Pratt and Viroque Baker 49; Marvin Rand 40, 93, 94, 95, 96, 157; Julius Shulman 51, 58, 106, 107, 114, 115, 117, 118, 120, 121, 122, 123, 124, 130, 137, 141, 142, 150, 151; Bancroft Library, University of California, Berkeley 36; W. P. Woodcock 92, 99, 111, 112, 127, 129, 131, 134. Ill. 3 is taken from *Einige Skizzen, Projekte und ausgeführte Bauwerke* by Otto Wagner (Vienna 1905); the photograph reproduced as Ill. 16 was taken by Schindler himself.

Preface

'The case of Schindler I do not profess to understand. There is certainly immense vitality, perhaps somewhat lacking among many of the best architects of the Pacific Coast. But this vitality seems in general to lead to arbitrary and brutal effects. Even his work of the last few years reminds one inevitably of the extreme Expressionist and Neo-Plastic work of the mid-twenties. Schindler's manner does not seem to mature. His continued reflection of the somewhat hectic psychological air of the region, from which all the others have attempted to protect themselves, still produces something of the look of sets for a Wellsian "film of the future".'

Thus I wrote in 1940 concerning the work of Schindler, which I did not know very well. On the whole, these few sentences may bear repeating thirty years later to introduce this monograph. I should hardly write in quite the same terms today: for example, the word 'Brutal' has since come to have a quite specific meaning in the criticism of modern architecture, and it does not apply to Schindler. But above all, I would now note what Mr Gebhard has developed so excellently at length. With the change in attitude towards modern architecture that has taken place over the last generation, the rigidity, the purism with which modern architecture was still being evaluated in the thirties has given way to a far more relaxed attitude towards it. One may say that where the references to Expressionism and 'films of the future' were certainly pejorative in 1940, they express rather well today some of the directions in which modern architecture has been moving since the last war. Of that movement Schindler's work, already from the beginning of his productive career in the mid-twenties, was by its very variety premonitory.

Speaking more strictly as a historian, I would note the extra-ordinary fact that, at the time, the significance of Schindler's achievement in the Lovell house was so little recognized. Designed in 1922, the year of Le Corbusier's Maison Citrohan project, the Lovell house now seems in retrospect one of the really crucial examples of the new architecture of the 1920s. Mr Gebhard has properly noted similarities and differences in relation to the work of Dutch architects of the twenties. He finds a sort of Neo-Plasticism the recurrent element in Schindler's long career. It is by no means the only theme that Schindler developed, however, as he drew upon his personal background in Wagner's Vienna and his association with Frank Lloyd Wright.

Architects of central European origin have played a con-siderable part in the history of American building, from Leopold Eidlitz in the mid-nineteenth century to the two Viennese – for a time working together – Schindler and Neutra, who are especially associated with the Los Angeles area. Happily, Mr Gebhard knows well the southern California scene: thus he is able to place Schindler's work in relation to its specific American milieu and thereby, perhaps, to propose a significant, if not a full, appreciation of those aspects of Schindler's work that once found so little acceptance from critics of the Eastern Seaboard such as myself. I am glad that this Foreword gives me an opportunity to make some redress for the narrow-minded approach to Schindler, and indeed to modern architecture in California more generally, of a generation ago.

H.-R. Hitchcock, London, 1971

CHAPTER ONE

New Worlds and Old

Rudolph Schindler and Los Angeles are one and inseparable. Until Los Angeles was (reluctantly) seen as *the* city of the present, it was impossible to sense what Schindler was about. In turn Los Angeles could not be 'discovered' until the fashion for the International Style and formal city planning was no longer stylish or 'smart'. Complexity, ambiguity, contradiction are the ingredients of Schindler's architecture, just as they are the guts and substance of the new city. Planning, visual and non-visual, can only exist in fragments, not as a whole. This is what Schindler's architecture is about, and so too is Los Angeles.

What sort of scene did the Vienna-trained Schindler find when he came to California in 1920? The population of the City of the Angels was 580,000; Hollywood, where Schindler was to live for the rest of his life, could boast only 36,000 inhabitants. Los Angeles even then was anything but a typical American city. Physically it was not a unified city: it was composed of distinct entities – Hollywood, Santa Monica, Pasadena – which were separated from one another by acres of open land, citrus groves and bean fields. Downtown Los Angeles might have been the pride of a city of, say, 200,000, but it was no longer scaled for a city of over half a million.

Before the First World War all of these disparate communities had been loosely held together by the electric railroad, but by 1920 the private automobile had already begun to usurp the railroad's primacy. By the middle of the decade Los Angeles County was far in the lead in the number of automobile registrations *per capita*.

Like others before and after, the Schindlers found it easy to settle into the man-made environment of Southern California.

9

2 A residential district of Los Angeles about 1920

Newcomers, as always, outnumbered the 'natives'. With the emergence in the twenties of the motion picture and oil industries, the capital of the 'Southland' began to assume a permanent, albeit rather eccentric, cosmopolitan character. Since the communities which composed Los Angeles were to all intents and purposes new, they conveyed the feeling (rightly or wrongly) that they welcomed the new, the progressive and the unusual. It was this atmosphere, plus the radically different physical and climatic environment, which encouraged Schindler

– and for a brief period Wright – to work in Los Angeles. By 1920 the receptivity to progressive architectural ideas was just about extinguished in Chicago and the Middle West. The West Coast was the only region in the United States which seemed to offer a sympathetic environment for non-traditional values and ideas. Schindler and Wright soon discovered that this openness to the genuinely new in the sphere of high art was only skin deep; yet it is doubtful if either of them could have done as well in any other section of the country.

Though Schindler's coming to California was directly due to his association with Wright, the notebooks he kept during his travels in the West in 1915 show that the Southland had already intrigued him. A similar fascination drew and held other central Europeans – Kem Weber, J.R. Davidson and Richard J. Neutra – to Los Angeles. By 1930, this Austro-German contingent pretty well dominated avant-garde design in Southern California. In a second-hand manner, Schindler and the others had been sympathetically exposed to California's architecture, especially the Mission Revival, through illustrations published in European books and magazines between 1900 and 1913. For a young Viennese already conditioned by Adolf Loos' idealized view of the United States and its technology, California must have seemed an Arcadia realized and unrealized.

'Modern Architecture', wrote Schindler in 1934, 'started with Mackintosh in Scotland, Otto Wagner in Vienna and Louis Sullivan in Chicago.' By the time he was thirty Schindler had to one degree or another experienced the buildings and ideas of all three. The designs of Mackintosh and the Glasgow group, as well as of Voysey and Baillie Scott, were known to him as a student in Vienna. If in the early 1900s an architect were to have picked the ideal place to acquire a progressive education, it would have been either Vienna or Berlin. In Vienna there was a constellation of talent unequalled in any other place. Wagner, Hoffmann, Loos and Olbrich were all there, or close by. These architects were paralleled in the world of painting by Klimt, Kokoschka and Schiele. Vienna's uniqueness was due not simply to a remarkable gathering of talent, but even more to the way in which this talent functioned. In varying degrees the outstanding figures worked both inside and outside the conservative establishment.

In his early years in Vienna Schindler followed a similar path. His youth was staid, respectable and middle-class. His parents were Viennese bourgeois. His father started as a furniture maker, spent a year in New York and when he returned established an import business. Schindler was born in Vienna on 5 September 1887. From his own description, his childhood seems to have been uneventful. He had one sister. After the usual preparatory schooling, culminating in the Gymnasium, he entered the Imperial Institute of Engineering in 1906 at the age of nineteen. In 1910, a year before he graduated from the Institute, he enrolled in the Vienna Academy of Fine Arts. Thus when he graduated from the Academy in 1913 he had acquired an academic background in both engineering and architecture which made an impressive dossier. Although its curriculum was outwardly stodgy and formal, the Academy under Wagner's direction was remarkably open and free. Schindler could certainly never have submitted his unconventional thesis or other designs at one of the Beaux Arts-oriented architectural schools in the United States at this period. Paralleling his studies was his work as a draughtsman in the office of Hans Mayr and Theodor M. Mayer. He worked for them from September 1911 to February 1914.

In the high art world of painting, Klimt, Kokoschka and Schiele exerted a strong influence on the younger students of the Academy, and Schindler took over many of their mannerisms in his figurative drawings. Loos too, although he held no post in the Academy, was admired and imitated by the students. Through him and through the publication by Wasmuth in 1910 of a portfolio by Frank Lloyd Wright, Schindler and his fellow students were made keenly aware of the technical and formal innovations then occurring in American architecture. The rapid dissemination of the Wasmuth portfolio of Wright is one of the really remarkable and still inadequately studied episodes in the history of modern architecture. By 1912 copies of the portfolio had been seen by young architectural students all over the Continent and across the Channel in England. For Schindler and his contemporaries Wright's Prairie architecture had a reality which was more alive and vital than any buildings which they knew at first hand. The impact of Wright's designs was due not only to the originality of their form, but equally to Wright's superb appreciation of what was needed in the way of presentation. His decision to rely solely on drawings made it possible for him to control fully what the viewer experienced via the two-dimensional page. In its essentials the Wasmuth portfolio was a theoretical treatise, which relied on drawings rather than the printed word. This volume, Wagner's *Modern Architecture*, and Loos' *Ornament and Crime* were the main theoretical baggage which Schindler had collected and carried with him when he left for the United States.

Schindler's student projects – like those of many of his contemporaries and, indeed, like the buildings of their professor Wagner – were fundamentally a stripped-down version of classical architecture. Schindler's stripped designs tend to be elegant in the manner of Wagner and Hoffmann; they are not outwardly aggressive as are most of Loos' buildings. In his project for a hunting lodge of 1912, Schindler made use of a classical U plan with a two-storey pavilion forming the base and dominating the composition. Vertical exposed steel beams replace the expected classical columns. Although sheathed in modular thin sheets of stone (like Wagner's work), the building was to be constructed of reinforced concrete. The visual quality of its surfaces and volumes is Rococo, as if an eighteenth-century drawing room had simply been turned inside out.

Similar modular panelling clothed the exterior of his 'Hotel Rong' (perhaps a pun on 'wrong'/'ring'?), a project of 1912. That this design relies heavily on the work of Wagner is apparent. Its basic form resembles Wagner's apartment house on Dobergasse of 1909–11; while the glass pavilion cantilevered out from the roof trellis is similar to the pavilion on the river side of Wagner's Lock house of 1906–7. Schindler's design, though, is less academic than the work of Wagner. The horizontal rows of the metal railings, together with the slim projecting floor slabs of the balconies, not only break up the surface of the building but, by declaring the existence of each of the

3   OTTO WAGNER Apartment house on Dobergasse, Vienna, 1909–11

4   Project for 'Hotel Rong',
Vienna, 1912

floor levels, help to project the interior space outward through
the hinged glass doors which lead on to each of the balconies.
At the base of the building, the glass sheathing of the ground
floor and the mezzanine suggests that the skin and skeleton of
the building are quite separate. Schindler's later fondness for
interlocking rectangular volumes and surfaces is anticipated in
the projection of the first floor balcony beyond the ends of the
upper balconies, and in the screen of panels which are extended
into the glass area.

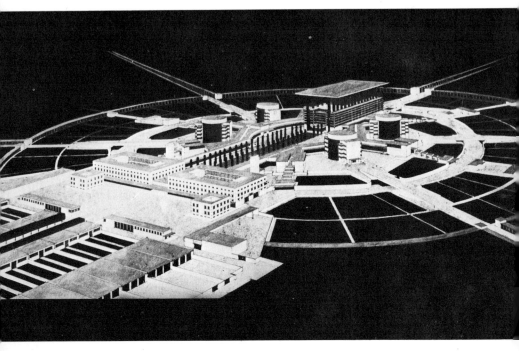

5   Project for a crematorium and chapel, Vienna, 1912–13

5, 6   Schindler's thesis project of 1912–13 for the Academy is a wild mixture of visual ideas. The subject of the thesis, a Crematorium and Chapel, and the grandiose scale of the project are typical of the paper world of the Beaux Arts. The gathering together of these components into the single concept of a circle harks directly back to the late eighteenth-century ideal-rationalist world of Ledoux and Boullée. Since the project itself has no relation to reality, the arbitrariness of its super-imposed geometry can at least partially be explained as symbolic. For the later Schindler and for modern architecture, it was the individual parts which were to count, not the overall scheme. The only feature of the site plan worth noticing is the inclusion of a sunken, inner circular road, with overpasses and inter-

16

changes. Compared to, say, Sant'Elia's project for a Futurist city of approximately the same date, Schindler's design is restrained and academic. Yet in its details Schindler's scheme comes far closer to the realities of planning today than does the science fiction wörld of Sant'Elia. This is true not only of the road patterns, but also of the relationship of the buildings. The major features of the plan are four towers and a dominant central structure separated by open spaces from low buildings of one or two storeys, thus providing both visual variety and light and air.

In design the individual buildings alternate between the way-out and the academic. All the buildings are symmetrically balanced, either within themselves or by being paired off against reverse but identical structures. In approved Beaux Arts fashion the buildings are also axially oriented to each other, either on the main north-south east-west axes or along spokes radiating from the hub of the circle. The two courtyard blocks paralleling and facing the entrance plaza are a pure and simple expression of stripped architecture. The four tower units, with the circular shape of their centres and their narrow horizontal window bands, could be mistaken for products of the Streamlined Moderne of the thirties. The low single-storey buildings located along the outer edges of four of the spoke roads, with their groups of windows placed directly under the roof slabs, anticipate not only the qualities of the International Style and of the Streamlined Moderne, but specifically such projects as Schindler's own Korsen Court of 1921. (They also bear a remarkable similarity to Neutra's work of the thirties.)

The central and dominant 'chapel' is a remarkably mature statement of Schindler's view – later asserted in the Lovell beach house – that the structure and enclosed volumes should be read as distinct and separate entities. A heavily projecting roof of steel beams and reinforced concrete is supported by two rows of thirty-two columns. The complex pattern of steel beams and rafters and concrete slab roof is fully exposed underneath, where it would be seen. Some distance beneath the roof he placed the enclosed space of the chapel. Its elementarist structure – like a child's building set (a suggestion of Froebel?) – was intended to be independent of the roof and its vertical supports. Here Schindler realized one part of his Manifesto, written when he was working on this project in 1912: 'the building's framework is no longer a symbol, it has become form itself.'

7   Schindler's one European building, the Clubhouse for Actors in Vienna (1912), was built while he was a draughtsman in the firm of Mayr and Mayer. It is a building which today could easily pass unnoticed. The upper part of its façade is typical Viennese 1900 with its slight references to classical panelling (almost Rococo), its pediments and projecting cornice. Only the row of slightly curved windows on the ground level gently suggests the work of Loos and Wagner. For Schindler, the importance of the Clubhouse was the practical experience it gave him in designing and then supervising the construction of a moderate sized building. His responsibility for this building (and the consequent letters of recommendation from Mayr and Mayer) were of great help when he applied for a position in the United States.

Like other young Viennese architects and architectural students, Schindler fell first under the spell of Wagner and only later under that of Loos; but in the long run (for good or bad) it was Loos who had the more deep and lasting effect on him. The religious intensity of the older man's commitment to architecture as 'high art', and to its relevance for his own existence and for life in general, was fully absorbed by Schindler. Like other European figures of the Modern Movement, Loos dragged into the twentieth century the view of Ruskin and Morris that architectural questions were in their essence moral questions – that one should judge architecture neither in strictly utilitarian terms nor in terms of visual style, but morally. While this evangelism (with its built-in arrogance) had its positive value, it had serious disadvantages, especially in the case of Schindler. He found it difficult to sell himself and his product in his adopted world of Southern California, even

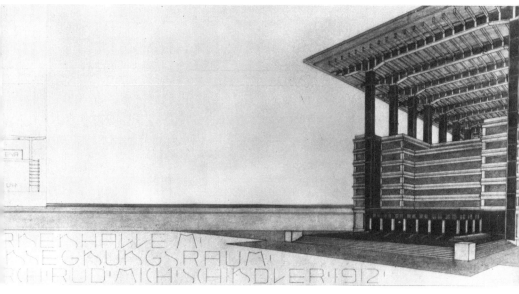

6 Project for a crematorium and chapel, Vienna, 1912–13: the chapel

though he was – perhaps more than any other architect – eventually able to unite the high and low art worlds of Southern California into one symbolic package.

Schindler does not seem to have been particularly impressed by stripped buildings, but he was intrigued by Loos' manipulation of interior space. Schindler was one of the few to see that the Loos interior was not only layered space: it was, even more, a vertical space. Loos' view that interior space should be thought of as a series of vertically related horizontal platforms was a theme which Schindler was to return to again and again. The most immediate and direct effect of all this on Schindler was to encourage him to go to America, which he already knew at second hand through his father's work there. Loos had presented an appealing picture of American technology, of its superb tools and of its varied building technology, particularly steel skeletal construction.

7 Clubhouse for Actors, Vienna, 1912

CHAPTER TWO

American apprenticeship

With Loos' encouragement Schindler answered an advertise-
ment by the Chicago firm of Henry A. Ottenheimer, Stern and
Reichert. He was selected from several applicants because of his
office experience with Mayr and Mayer and his dual degrees in
engineering and architecture, plus the fact that he was then a
skilled draughtsman. With funds provided by the Chicago firm,
Schindler sailed for America in June 1914, just before the out-
break of the First World War. His original plans were to complete his three-year contract with Ottenheimer, Stern and
Reichert; then work for a year or two with Frank Lloyd Wright
and travel as much as he could, before returning to Vienna to
work for Loos. The thought of eventually returning to Vienna
remained with him even after he came to California; but the
reality of going back became increasingly remote. The European war made it dangerous and even impossible to try to
return. With America's entry into the war in 1917 Schindler
found himself an enemy alien. After 1919 the post-war scene
in central Europe was grim; even with Loos as City Architect,
the immediate prospects for work in Vienna were discouraging.
Schindler's marriage in 1919 to Pauline Gibling, with her
intense involvement in social and political problems, and then
the impact of Southern California, finally made the idea of
returning to Europe completely unreal.

The firm in which Schindler spent his first years, that of
Ottenheimer, Stern and Reichert, was a successful Chicago
office. The chief partner, Henry A. Ottenheimer, had been a
draughtsman with Adler and Sullivan and had attended the
Ecole des Beaux-Arts in Paris. The firm had a reputation in the
Chicago business community for keeping to estimates and for
sound construction. They were not passionately committed on

the stylistic 'packaging' of their structures. Although much of their work was of the commonest classicism after McKim, Mead and White, a number of their designs were obviously influenced by Sullivan's work of the nineties. Their office offered Schindler just the sort of practical experience he most needed. For here was an active firm of moderate size where he could work on a variety of projects, including that form which the Europeans most admired, the skyscraper. Here he could apply his theoretical engineering knowledge and his own design concepts to buildings which he could see being built.

In their outward form the buildings of Chicago in 1914 were a mixed bag. The commercial tradition of Sullivan was moribund, and even Wright's domestic Prairie mode was on the wane. In spite of the presidency of Woodrow Wilson there was a general decline in all forms of liberalism. Frontier innocence was fast becoming remote, and the stern latter-day morality of the Arts and Crafts movement – which produced, among other things, the California bungalow – was being supplanted by more sophisticated and light-hearted ideas and forms. Both in the Midwest and on the West Coast, progressive architecture had tied itself so closely to the simple, honest life of the Arts and Crafts movement, which was a nineteenth-century product, that it could not revamp either its ideology or its aesthetics.

Technologically, Chicago architecture of 1914 was as advanced as ever. The only thing which had really changed was the style of its buildings; and the attiring of a skyscraper in classical or Gothic garb was only marginally less functional than the packaging provided by Sullivan and his followers. Admittedly the Midwestern, middle-class suburban houses of the war years and of the twenties were less appealing in their visual form than the houses of Wright and Purcell and Elmslie, but in many ways they were far more habitable. They were environments built for comfort and as such they incorporated the latest in heating, plumbing and other mechanical devices. Since the designers of these houses, whether builders or architects, were not trying to prove a point, they found it easy to incorporate the latest technical device or to reorganize their surface to respond to the latest fashion. What made the houses modern was their mechanical core, not their styling.

Schindler responded with enthusiasm to Chicago. Soon after coming he bought a small camera (which he never learned to use correctly) and proceeded to record the Chicago scene – not so much specific buildings as more general schemes. He avidly read the major architectural journals, cutting out the articles and illustrations which interested him and taking copious notes from others. He did not concern himself with form, but with the structural and mechanical aspects of building – what equipment (heating, lighting, elevators, and so on) was needed for an urban office building or large hotel, what the utilitarian space needs of these larger buildings were, and how these were assembled. The academic classical envelopes which clothed these structures did not seem to bother him one way or the other; he seems simply to have ignored them.

As in his student days in Vienna, Schindler began to attend life drawing classes (at the Palette and Chisel Club), and to participate in the meetings and exhibitions of the Chicago

8   Pencil and crayon drawing, Chicago, 1914/18

Architectural Club. All of his figurative drawings known today date from his first years in Chicago, and are similar in style to those he had produced between 1910 and 1914 in Vienna. Their source was the drawings, watercolours and paintings of Klimt
8, 9 and Schiele. Schindler of course was not alone in taking over this mode; for these two painters were the idols of all of the younger progressive Viennese students, and the figurative drawings of Neutra reflect the same influence. Particularly in Schiele, the agitation of the late Secessionist-Art Nouveau line was played off against occasional cubist geometric patterns. Schindler took up this theme, but the results, as one would expect, are quite different. The swift-moving line of Schiele became tightly controlled in Schindler's hand; and instead of using it to define a living form, he constructed static, architectural volumes. The one strong point of similarity between Schindler and Schiele is the manner in which the flat two-dimensional rectangular or linear patterns are ambiguously contrasted with the traditionally built up volumes of the figures. Most of Schindler's drawings are of the female nude – either the entire figure or a detail. These figures are neither enticing, nor erotic; they are fascinating but slightly repulsive.

Only a few months after his arrival in 1914 Schindler entered the design competition for a neighbourhood centre, sponsored by the Chicago Architectural Club. His two perspective
10 drawings are Wrightian and Japanesque. The sheets of parchment paper are long and narrow, and he employs a technique of perspective lacking a horizon line. The drawings are in coloured ink with much of their background filled in with gold. The lettering and vertical line of squares and rectangles are Wrightian. At the lower left can be seen one of the first uses of Schindler's monogram, derived from Schiele and Wright.

As a two-dimensional composition, his drawing for the neighbourhood centre is far more handsome and accomplished than the drawings for his thesis. As architecture, however, it is far more academic. The individual buildings depicted in the neighbourhood centre are closer to his 1912 designs for the

24

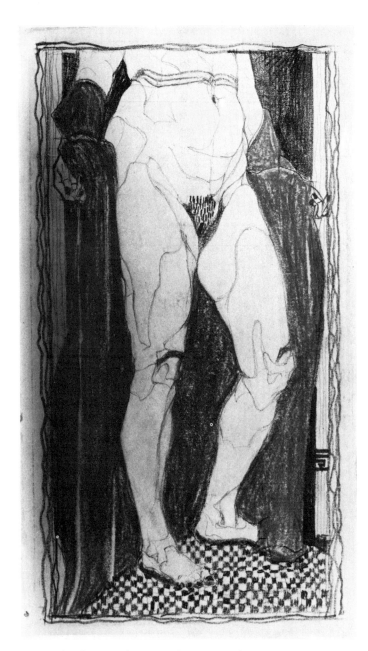

9　Pencil and crayon drawing, Chicago, 1914/15

26

Hotel Rong and the hunting lodge. The only points of strong similarity between his thesis scheme and the neighbourhood centre are the multi-level walks and the pedestrian overpasses which project over the main street intersecting the site.

In addition to his day-to-day draughting and engineering activities at the Ottenheimer, Stern and Reichert office, Schindler designed and produced the presentation drawings for several projects which were not built. The most interesting of these are an eleven-storey hotel and a bar for a hotel, both of 1915. The hotel is a simple vertical rectangular volume of red brick; its surface is punctured by rows of steel and glass bay windows, one to each room. The project for a bar harks back to Loos' cafés and bars in Vienna.

Late in the summer of 1915, Schindler made a long trip by train to New Mexico, Arizona and California. As with many others who have visited the area, he was deeply affected by the vernacular adobe architecture of the upper Rio Grande Valley.

◀ 10 Design for a
neighbourhood
centre, Chicago,
1914

11 Sketch made in
   northern New
   Mexico, 1915

1915

A COUNTRY HOME
IN ADOBE CONSTR
FOR DR T P MARTIN
TAOS NEW MEXICO
R M SCHINDLER ARCH

12, 13   Projected 'country
home in adobe' for
T. P. Martin, Taos,
New Mexico, 1915:
opposite, general view;
right, plan

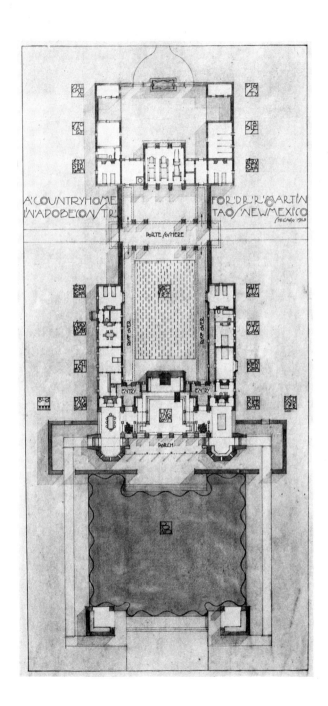

He took numerous photographs of buildings in Santa Fe and
11 in Taos and recorded others in pencil sketches. In a way, his
sympathetic response to these thick-walled, primitive structures illustrates the internal contradiction which many figures
of the Modern Movement have felt between their ideological
beliefs and their emotive response to visual forms. In his 1912
Manifesto Schindler had written, 'our efficient way of using
materials eliminated the plastic structural mass'; and yet in his
12 1915 project for the Martin house at Taos he sculpted a form in
traditional adobe. His scheme for the Martin house shows at
an early point in his career his willingness to modify or completely throw off parts of his theoretical baggage if they got in
the way of his design process. In the plan of the Martin house,
13 he united New Mexican folk architecture with Wright, Loos
and the Beaux Arts. The courtyard layout, with rooms and
corridors opening along the interior roofed porches, was
entirely traditional in the area. The balanced symmetry of the
scheme – like so much of Wright's Prairie work – is Beaux
Arts, while the relationship between the living room, the
connecting dining room and billiard room and the double
entrances is pure Wright. The change of floor levels, with the
projection of platforms into the lowered space of the living
room, is derived from Loos. In the Martin project one finds
Schindler's first open acceptance of contradiction as a positive
quality of design. Interior space is at one moment opened to
the outside, at the next closed off. Large plate glass 'picture'
windows in the dining and billiard rooms extend the interior
outward, while the alcoves in each of these rooms, with their
narrow slit windows, are close to being secluded caves.

After his Rio Grande experience Schindler travelled to
California, where he visited the Pan Pacific Expositions in San
Francisco and San Diego, before going on to Los Angeles. His
notes and sketches do not indicate that he was in any way as
enthusiastic about California (at this time) as he had been about
New Mexico. He photographed Mullgardt's buildings at the
San Francisco Fair and Goodhue's at San Diego, and he recorded

a number of Mission Revival buildings and San Diego houses by Irving Gill. He did not mention, sketch or photograph any of the buildings of Charles and Henry Greene, nor for that matter did the California bungalow seem to interest him.

The rest of Schindler's designs of 1916–17, accomplished after he returned to Chicago and before he started working full time for Wright, followed two separate paths. His designs for Ottenheimer, Stern and Reichert were all for buildings in Chicago – a new store front on Van Buren Street (*c.* 1916), and projects for a central administration building (1916), for the Homer Emunim Temple and School (1915–16), and for one-room apartments (1919), and the Buena Shore Club (1917–18) – and in these he carried on with no major changes the forms he had developed in Vienna. His smaller buildings and projects, however – the projects for a 'Log House' (1916–17), and for a women's club in Chicago (1916), and his remodelling of the J.B. Lee house at Maywood (1916) – are experiments in Wright's Prairie mode.

In form the Homer Emunim Temple and School is a single cube, more sculptural in character than volumetric. In contrast, the projected administration building, with its rows of double-hung windows and its sheathing of brick below and stucco above, is anything but monumental; what Schindler did here in

14

15–17

18

19

14

14 Project for the Homer Emunim Temple and School, Chicago, 1915–16

fact was simply to reorganize the vocabulary of the run-of-the-mill commercial vernacular. The Buena Shore Club exhibited characteristics from both of these projected buildings. It had a steel frame, supplemented by reinforced concrete and walls of hollow tile. In some areas Schindler left the surface of the hollow tile exposed so that it would provide a tactile contrast to the white stucco walls. With its L-shaped rectangular blocks and its heavy vertical detailing, it parallels avant-garde Dutch work of the late teens and early twenties. Some features, particularly the narrow horizontal bands of windows carried around corners, seem to be lifted straight from Schindler's 1912–13 thesis; while the group of high angular bay windows facing the garden and the lake are related to the Loosian bays of his 1912 Clubhouse for Actors. The long, low wing which houses the dining room is loosely Wrightian, especially the row of squat triangular columns which taper sharply at the top.

The last project which Schindler prepared for Ottenheimer, Stern and Reichert was a twelve-storey tower of one-room flats (1919). The plan of each apartment, with its separate bathroom, kitchenette, and main room divided into living and dining area, is tight and compact. Though Schindler used glass walls and doors between dining area, kitchenette, hall and bath, the interior would never have been satisfactorily lit by the single triple window at the end of the living room. Stylistically the arrangement of the fenestration and sheathing of the exterior is remarkable. The triple window of each apartment is set in a deep picture-like frame, and these frames are arranged in vertical rows with a single sheet of glass separating the ends of the frame. The remaining wall surface is sheathed in thin modular slabs of precast concrete.

Before joining Wright, Schindler had produced several designs which placed him for a brief moment among the architects of the Prairie School. The first of these was for a small summer vacation house, which he simply labelled a 'Log House'. It was designed in 1916, and the drawings were finished at Taliesin the following year. The scheme of a symmetrical

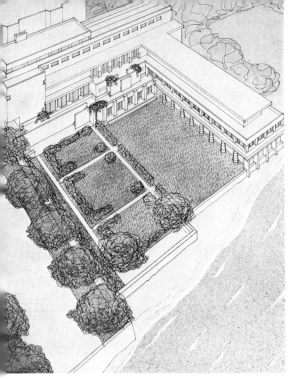

15, 16   Buena Shore Club, Chicago, 1917–18: above, view from lake; below, view from garden courtyard (a photograph by Schindler)

17   Project for one-room apartments, Chicago, 1919: top, plans of two apartments; above, elevation

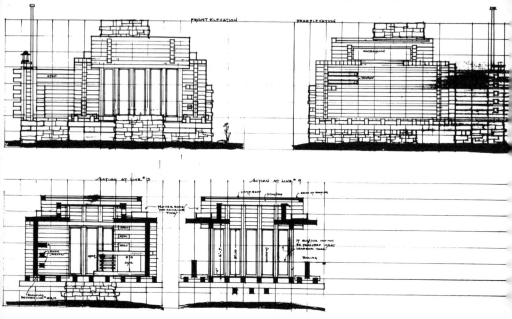

18 Project for a 'Log House', 1916–17: above, elevations; below, cross-sections

pavilion with interlocking smaller volumes was of course Wrightian in flavour. But the way in which Schindler related his volumes was much more sculptural than most of Wright's designs of the Prairie years. By suspending the log-enclosed volume on recessed or projecting stone piers, Schindler makes the building float above the ground in a manner that is non-Wrightian (although it foreshadows Wright's Kaufmann house of 1936). Also non-Wrightian in its intensity is the self-conscious declaration of the log structure. Schindler not only thrusts the ends of the logs far out beyond the corners, he makes the floor joists and ceiling rafters plainly visible. His narrow horizontal windows are simply open spaces where the logs have been removed. Thin band windows of an almost identical type were to appear again as a direct response to structure in Schindler's Pueblo Ribera Court of 1923. Shortly after coming to Chicago Schindler had become intrigued with modular planning: the design of the log house is the outgrowth of his horizontal and vertical use of a four foot module, which he was to employ, with minor refinements, in most of his later work.

47

34

19 Remodelled house for J. B. Lee, Maywood, Illinois, 1916

Schindler's transformation of the small commonplace farm
dwelling of J. B. Lee at Maywood (1916) into a Prairie house   *19*
produced an unorthodox building. The existing interior was
gutted and completely rearranged, with the lower floor becoming a single large living space. On the upper floor the bedrooms
were regrouped and a bath was added. A large open porch
was added to provide more space on the ground floor, and new
dormers above provided more usable space and light. As in his
project for the log house, Schindler cantilevered the wooden
volume of the house so that it hovered over the site on its
stone piers.

The design for a women's club in Chicago (1916) is out-   *20*
spokenly Wrightian, similar to Dutch work of the late teens
and early twenties – Rob. van't Hoff's 1915 house near Utrecht
or J. J. P. Oud's project for a factory of 1919. Like his Dutch
contemporaries Schindler revised the Wrightian Prairie prototype so that its volumes and surfaces as they appear from outside are more completely governed by a manipulation of
rectangular geometric forms. Schindler's form, however, is

35

much looser than that of the Europeans, for in this design he is perfectly willing to contrast rectangular geometry with a low, double-pitched roof (reminiscent of an American barn) covering the auditorium of the club on the upper floor. Also in contrast to the Europeans, Schindler did not disregard many of the subtleties of Wright's planning: a double corner entrance (visible to the left in the drawing) leads into a tree-shaded courtyard; alternative paths (doors and staircases) lead off the entrance courtyard; interior space is both opened and closed, vertically and horizontally.

20   Project for a women's club, Chicago, 1916: street elevation

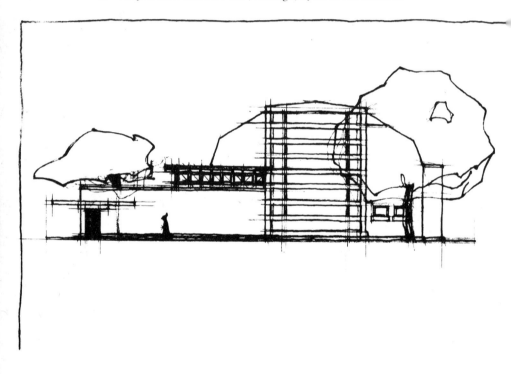

CHAPTER THREE

The years with Wright

Schindler had approached Wright about the possibility of working for him a number of times, the earliest being in 1916. America's entrance into the war in 1917 and the intensity of the anti-German mood in the United States made Schindler's life unpleasant. Since there was no real alternative to remaining in America, he continued to plead with Wright to employ him, which Wright finally did in 1917. Schindler's asset was his engineering background, for Wright needed help to complete the working drawings for the Imperial Hotel in Tokyo, especially in developing its complex floating foundation. Schindler, like others (such as Walter Burley Griffin) who had worked for Wright previously, ended up by being not only a structural engineer, but an office accountant, a building super-intendent and a designer, as well as being involved in the day-to-day life and activities of Taliesin. What Wright's reaction to Schindler really was during these years is difficult to determine. He must have had some respect for his abilities, for otherwise he would not have given him the responsibility for the com-pletion of several designs and the supervision of such an important commission as the Hollyhock House. Much later, in 1932, in his *Autobiography*, Wright wrote that 'Rudy Schindler was too smooth a party ever to learn how to be serious, which is the reason why I liked him.'

The part played by Schindler in the designs which came from the Wright office is difficult to ascertain. If one takes into account Wright's inventive ability and his operatic ego-centricity (a characteristic Schindler later adopted), it is really unthinkable that he would allow anyone working for him to be fully responsible for any project. One must posit that the core of each scheme was solely Wright's. If he was in Japan, as

THE
MONOLITH
HOME

Rudolph Schindler
FIRST SKETCH
OAK PARK 1919

21   WRIGHT AND SCHINDLER Project for a concrete 'Monolith Home', 1919

was frequently the case during the years 1917 to 1921, Schindler
(or later the architect's son, Lloyd Wright) might modify this
or that detail. Thus although the house for Mrs J. P. Shampay
in Chicago (1919) is a characteristic cruciform Prairie house, it
does exhibit several features which were probably Schindler's.
The rearrangement of the cruciform plan to contain a garage
next to the main entrance door is the sort of thing that Schindler
was fond of doing in the twenties. The simplification of surfaces
and the way in which volumes penetrate one another are the
type of changes that a person might make who had initially
been inspired by the perspective drawings of the 1910 Wasmuth

38

portfolio. The C. E. Staley house at Waukegan (1919) shows a similar departure from Wright's Prairie schemes – the driveway and the garage which serve as the main approach and entrance, and a central hall which serves both as the main entrance and as a bedroom hall, and a large pleasant kitchen for the use of the family rather than the servants (something seldom found in Wright's work, or for that matter in Schindler's own designs of the twenties and thirties).

As Henry-Russell Hitchcock has pointed out, one of the most significant of Wright's works in the period 1910–20 was the project for a 'Workmen's Colony of Concrete Monolith Homes' at Racine, Wisconsin (1919). Wright must certainly *21* have worked out the general scheme, as it again anticipated his precast concrete block houses of the twenties. But the stark stripped-down rectangularity of the geometry, in the details as well as in the relationship of the volumes, could have been Schindler's contribution. If one looks at Wright's and Schindler's work of the twenties, it is Schindler's Pueblo Ribera Court *47* which comes the closest to the forms of the monolithic houses.

Schindler's three Prairie designs reveal numerous internal conflicts between his functional, informal planning and his aesthetic need to enclose space in a complex geometry of forms. Wright had similar difficulties, but in his case one always feels that utilitarian considerations will be sacrificed to form. With Schindler the opposite was the case: aesthetics are in some measure sacrificed to utility.

The planning for Olive Hill, Los Angeles, offered Wright the opportunity of designing an urban scheme of some size – something he had always longed for, but had not been able to do. Here was an entire hill on the edge of a growing urban area. The owner, Aline Barnsdall, wished not only to build a residence for herself, but to provide a cultural centre for the growing Hollywood community. As conceived by the client, the scheme was to contain several individual houses, a theatre, studio apartments for painters, actors and writers and a group of terrace stores along Hollywood and Sunset Boulevards.

Aline Barnsdall, whose father had been an oil magnate, had a sizeable fortune; she was passionate about the theatre, and in politics was a 'parlour pink', just enough of a radical to upset the leaders of the Babbitt-oriented business community of Los Angeles.

Wright noted in writing about the house for Miss Barnsdall herself, Hollyhock House: 'It had been finally completed with great difficulty . . . partly because I had to leave it in amateur hands.' That Wright was not happy with the finished house is certain. Whether he felt in 1920 as he did in the thirties that it was Schindler's ineptness which had adversely affected the result is open to question. One can well imagine the built-in difficulties, particularly of personalities, which affected the Olive Hill project. Schindler found himself uncomfortably in the middle of a triumvirate composed of Wright, Aline Barnsdall and the contractor. Though helped by Lloyd Wright, who had joined his father in 1919, Schindler probably did not have the experience needed to run a building operation of this complexity. With Wright in Japan, Schindler had to make decisions which should have been made by Wright himself. In order to keep down the continually rising cost of the build-ing and also as an expression of his own philosophy of design, he eliminated and simplified numerous details. Miss Barnsdall had a sneaking suspicion that she was being conned by Wright, for she felt that the great man should have been interested enough in her project to be around during its construction. And as the house progressed she, like many of Wright's clients, found that the cost of the project continued to climb, both because of unforeseen constructional difficulties and because of changes which she insisted upon. She wanted the house to function really well and made changes to ensure its liveability. Like other clients of progressive twentieth-century architecture, she had a split reaction to the new building rising on her Holly-wood hill. To have a building by Wright was a notoriety she wished for, but at the same time she was not sure she really wished to live in a monument. As the Hollyhock House neared

22 Director's house, Olive Hill, Los Angeles, 1920

completion, it became all too apparent that it was much more of a monument than a house to be lived in. Schindler in his best manner tried to soothe the occasionally outraged feelings of the client. He was so successful that not only was the main house at last brought to completion, but Miss Barnsdall became his close friend and later one of his major clients.

Before Wright returned from Japan and before the Hollyhock House was finished, Schindler did the preliminary designs and the working drawings for the two other single-family houses which were built on Olive Hill. The drawings were sent to Japan, and Wright approved them, apparently without any changes. The buildings in question were the Director's house 22 and the Oleanders house (both 1920). The scheme for

41

Oleanders would appear to have been a joint design by Wright and Schindler. The Director's house, with its strange fusion of Wright's Prairie and Pre-Columbian modes, and its looser plan, must be credited to Schindler, for all of the initial sketches, finished designs and working drawings are by him. Neither before nor after did Wright in his concrete houses produce a plan such as this, nor did he ever design a house which so successfully brought together his Prairie and Pre-Columbian styles. The bedroom wing of the Director's house is in effect an open sleeping porch with walls of sliding windows on three sides. The dining and stair hall spaces overlook the double height living room (as in many of Wright's Prairie schemes and also in Le Corbusier's work of around 1920). The centre of the house is treated as a utility core with baths and kitchen and heating placed one above the other. The symmetry of individual surfaces and volumes is maintained on the exterior, but the interior plan weaves in and out in a free and easy fashion.

During 1920–22 (and even as late as 1923) Schindler continued to work for Wright. He did the drawings for a small 'temporary' one-room house for J. B. Irving at Wilmette (1920) and the working drawings for the unbuilt 'Actors' Abode' (apartments for actors) and the terrace stores for Olive Hill (1920). With the help of Lloyd Wright he produced the working drawings for the first of the precast concrete block houses, the Millard house at Pasadena (1922–3). Schindler worked on a variety of different schemes for the Eagle Rock house of C. P. Lowes. His first design for the Lowes house is a wood

23 frame, stucco-covered Prairie cruciform, with the eaves of the roof articulated by severe apron bands of horizontal overlaid redwood boards. The next scheme exhibits a plan close to Wright's later Storer house (1924), but the structure is of slip-form reinforced concrete, identical to that which Schindler

46 later used in the Pueblo Ribera Court in 1923 (this technique had been used earlier by Lloyd Wright). All of these schemes for the Lowes house were abandoned because they far exceeded the client's budget, and after Schindler left Wright he produced

23 First scheme for a house for C. P. Lowes, Eagle Rock, 1922

32 an equally interesting but much less expensive house for the Lowes family in 1923.

24 While still with Wright, Schindler unsuccessfully entered the competition for a Free Public Library, Bergen Branch, Jersey City, New Jersey (1920). Considering the intensity of Schindler's admiration for Wright at this time, it is surprising how few specifically Wrightian ideas enter into the library project. The only external hint of Wright is in the fenestration where an intricate rectangular pattern of mullions occurs to the left and right of the main windows. Perhaps it could be argued that the interior, where the secondary areas all open into the central three-storey space, is reminiscent of Wright's Unity Temple and Larkin Building. Yet within and without the enclosing surfaces and the volumes have been reduced to a simplified rectangular vocabulary more in the spirit of Le Corbusier's work of the twenties than of Wright. The concepts of window patterning, clerestory lighting and vertical interior space were all to crop up shortly in Schindler's house for Dr *59–61* Phillip Lovell at Newport Beach (1922–6), and in several other *51* projects of the mid-twenties, especially his Sachs apartments at Los Angeles (1926–40).

24   Project for a Free Public Library, Bergen Branch, Jersey City, New Jersey, 1920

CHAPTER FOUR

Opportunity : California in the twenties

Schindler's break with the Wright office and the setting up of his own private architectural practice was gradual. A good part of 1921 was devoted to his own projects, and by late 1922 he had completed his own house on Kings Road (1921–2) where he was to have his office until his death in 1953. By 1922 he and his wife had become an integral part of the Hollywood community, and he confidently expected to obtain enough independent commissions to make a living. He was also wary of Wright's overpowering personality. As he had written to a friend in 1919, 'Not one of Wright's men has yet found a word to say for himself.' It could be argued, as Schindler himself admitted, that he had already been too long with Wright. His attempt to combine the expressionist mood of Wright's architecture with the intellectual purism of Europe continued to produce ambiguity in much of his later work. Although conflicts such as this helped him to achieve a richness of detail and form, their effect was often negative. Schindler's obsession with Wright's work and personality, coupled with his own nineteenth-century romanticism, made it difficult for him to slough off casually his experience in the Wright office.

When the Schindlers and the engineer Clyde Chase built their two-family house on Kings Road the country to the west of Hollywood was still open land, occasionally broken up by bean fields. But the atmosphere (particularly for builders and architects) was that of a potential El Dorado. The population of Hollywood grew from 36,000 in 1920 to 235,000 by 1930; building was in progress all round. Hollywood, as the motion picture capital, was rapidly becoming both respectable (which it had not been) and rich; oil was bringing new wealth to the Southland (by now spelled with a capital S); and already the automobile was an essential of day-to-day life. Both before and during the thirties Los Angeles glittered with flamboyant personalities and ideas, from Aimee Semple McPherson's Four Square Gospel to the personification of political and social reaction in General Harrison Gray Otis (*d.* 1917), and those who carried on his point of view in the *Los Angeles Times* and in the anti-labour Merchants and Manufacturers Association. Here was the home of Upton Sinclair, the centre for Theosophists, nudists, naturopaths and health and body faddists, and the largest number of dog and cat hospitals (and cemeteries) to be found in any city in America. Notwithstanding the negative image of Los Angeles conveyed by Forest Lawn cemetery (established in 1917), by a long tradition of police terrorism and by the Cinderella world of Hollywood, the capital of the Southland has always had a strong pull as a Utopia. William Butler Yeats wrote, 'Here if anywhere else in America I seem to hear the coming footsteps of the muse.' Lord Bryce observed that Southern California conveyed 'a sort of consciousness of separate existence.' 'No notion', wrote Carey McWilliams in 1946, 'is more deeply seated, no idea has echoed more persistently through the years, than the theory that a new vital culture would someday be born in California.'

By 1919–20 Los Angeles was just beginning to embrace the Spanish Colonial Revival: by the end of the decade much of suburban Southern California had been transformed into a new synthetic version of the Mediterranean world. In theory, modern architects were utterly opposed to this borrowing of past architectural styles, but both Schindler and Neutra did try their hands at one or two exercises in a Spanish Colonial Revival; indeed by 1930 Schindler had borrowed quite a bit from both Mission and Spanish Colonial Revivals. Because of the high cost and constructional difficulties involved, Schindler gradually ceased to use concrete for his residential work. In its place he adopted the prevalent stucco-covered wooden stud frame. He ended up using stucco, just as the Los Angeles contractor-builder did, to cover everything from the fascias of eaves to the vertical and horizontal wooden members of a trellis. Such folksy Spanish Colonial Revival features as shed roofs, tile floors and tile roofs entered into his designs. Pueblo Ribera Court, his own house on Kings Road and the Popenoe cabin could, within reason, be labelled Pueblo Revival. During the twenties especially, he was fascinated by the bungalow court, a Southern California invention of 1908–10.

94, 96, 159

Schindler's house on Kings Road of 1921–2 and the Lovell beach house of 1922–6 are without question his masterpieces – a view shared by Schindler himself. They are in fact unique in Schindler's production, though certain of their features do crop up in several of his later buildings. As a radical rethinking of the whole man-made environment, the Kings Road house is the more original.

25–28, 159 55–57, 59–61

By the time Schindler had started the design for the Kings Road house they were to share with the Chases, he and his wife had formed a close friendship with the Lovells. Dr Phillip Lovell, editor of the popular 'Care of the Body' column regularly published in the *Los Angeles Times*, was an advocate of life in the out-of-doors, of physical exercise and of 'natural' unprocessed foods. He believed in a free and easy-going education for children (his own often played in the nude), and he wished to immerse himself and his family in all that was 'modern'. For Schindler, the architectural moralist, Lovell's passion for sunlight, ozone and hygiene was very appealing. The degree of Schindler's commitment can be sensed in a series of six articles on architecture and its relation to health which he contributed in 1926 to Dr Lovell's column. In these articles he expounded many of the thoughts which underlie the design of the Kings Road house: 'Our rooms', he wrote, 'will descend close to the ground and the garden will become an integral part of the house. The distinction between indoors and outdoors will disappear. Our house will lose its front-and-back-door aspect. It will cease being a group of dens, some larger ones for social effect, and a few smaller ones (bedrooms) in which to herd the family. Each individual will want a private room to gain a background for his life. He will sleep in the open. A work-and-playroom, together with the garden, will satisfy the group needs.' Schindler later wrote of his 'cooperative dwelling', 'This theme fulfils the basic requirements for a camper's shelter: a protected back, an open front, a fireplace and a roof.'

Schindler approached the 100 × 200 foot Kings Road lot as a single, enclosed environment. Every square foot was utilized to form some sort of spatial enclosure. Given the rapidity and ease of growing trees and hedges in Southern California, Schindler could create his outdoor living spaces with vegetation as easily as he could form them with walls of concrete, wood or canvas. Spatially he divided the lot into seven outdoor zones: a narrow, rather close, entrance path; a front patio-garden, which was integrated with the north part of the house; a second front patio-garden, associated with the south part of the house; a small patio facing the rear, which was an extension of the big room; an orchard enclosure; a hedged vegetable plot; and a service and driveway area. The roofed enclosed space expressed Schindler's view that each of the four occupants of the house should have a private retreat. A design studio (labelled 'R.M.S.' on the plans) was provided for his use; his wife's retreat (labelled 'S.P.G.') was in the centre; and two retreats for the Chases were placed in the northern part of the building. Each pair of retreats formed an L and opened on to an outdoor living room through sliding canvas doors which during the summer months could be completely removed. The two main outdoor living rooms were provided with their own fireplaces. A common kitchen was to be used jointly by the Schindlers and the Chases, the wives taking turns to cook so that the household tasks would not become repetitious for either. No bedrooms as such were provided, for the occupants were expected to sleep in the open in 'sleeping baskets' (i.e. sleeping porches) placed over each of the entrances.

As an environment for living, the Kings Road house is a peculiar mixture of nineteenth- and twentieth-century precepts. The romantic desire to live in the open – feeling the need

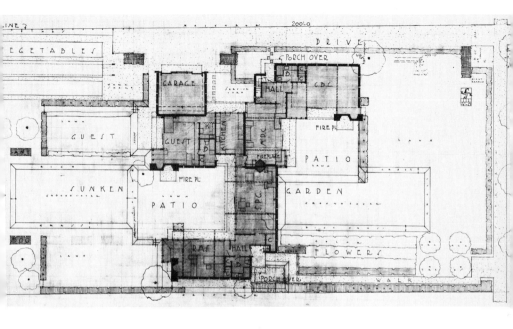

25, 26   House for Schindler and Clyde Chase, Kings Road, Hollywood, 1921–2:
above, plan; below, Schindler's studio (bottom centre on plan)

27, 28   House for Schindler
and Clyde Chase,
Kings Road, Hollywood,
1921–2: above, construction
of lift-slab walls; right,
the living room

to expose one's body to the rigours of nature – is a pure Arts and Crafts idea, in line with the masculine toughness of such American exponents of the Arts and Crafts as Elbert Hubbard and Gustav Stickley (and on the West Coast of Bernard Maybeck and the brothers Charles and Henry Greene). But Schindler's view of the outdoor life was European. His 'natural' environment was not the wild open spaces of the western frontier, but a small tightly controlled urban environment; and in this he was, like Le Corbusier and other exponents of modern architecture, wholly of the twentieth century. In a number of ways the Kings Road house was retrogressive for the twenties, particularly in its disregard for mechanical heating which by then had become an essential part of the American home. Herbert D. Croley, long associated with the *California Architect and Engineer*, wrote that 'Southern California is a country in which almost any kind of house is practical and almost any kind of a plant will grow': but while the Southern California climate is indeed mild, it does have its ups and downs of cold, dampness and heat. Schindler aimed for the norm, ignored the extremes, and in the process compromised the full liveability of his environment.

The structure of the house, like its environment, was a bundle of opposites. The concrete floor and the concrete tilt-slab walls (derived indirectly from Irving Gill's work through *27* Lloyd Wright) were experimental and advanced – particularly for the West Coast. The repetitive slab walls suggested modern technology, and their rhythmic appearance throughout the *26, 159* house expressed the repetitive process of machine production. In contrast to these concrete surfaces are the wooden ceilings, *28* with their narrow clerestory lighting, the thin internal walls of wood and the sliding doors, all of which strongly suggest impermanence. The house was, as Schindler had said, a marriage between the solid permanent cave and the open lightweight tent.

This cave-tent shelter of concrete, wood and canvas was repeated in three vacation houses – the cabin for Paul Popenoe at Coachella (1922 and 1924), the cabin for Phillip Lovell at Wrightwood (1924) and the ranch house for Carlton Park at Fallbrook (1925). Schindler's unwillingness to use the machine to modify the climate and environment worked far better in these vacation houses than in his own Hollywood house. All three were located in the dry inner valley between the coast and the central desert, and they were not meant to be used when the weather was either too cold or too hot.

29   He pursued a similar approach in a projected 'desert house', probably for P. Popinoff, designed around 1924 and probably intended for the semi-arid Palm Springs region. Like the Kings Road house, it is a designed environment, completely self-contained. The space enclosed by the thick concrete walls is really a protected, cool cave. The high-walled courtyard with

29   Project for a desert house, c. 1924

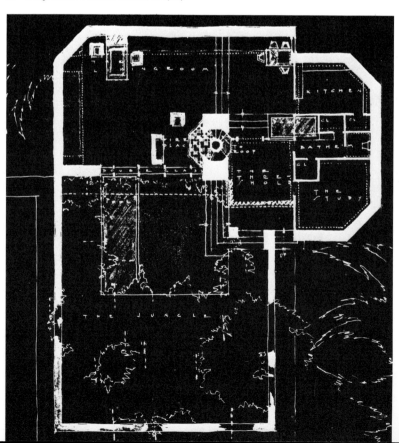

its partial roof, pool and jungle of vegetation is simply a limited extension of the more secluded enclosed space. Within, the house is essentially a single room; even the kitchen and the bath are mere alcoves, extensions of the main space. The utilitarian bath tub is transformed into a pool from which water flows through the house, down into the garden pool, and then overflows to water the plants.

The initial impact of the mild uncritical environment of Southern California both stimulated and deadened Schindler's response. It encouraged him to unite internal and external space meaningfully, and to revamp completely the accepted spatial divisions. The native use of adobe for walls was certainly one element which prompted him to use reinforced concrete in its natural state (not covered by stucco, as was usual in the work of Irving Gill). The limpid mildness of the normal climate, in which day-to-day life outdoors could really exist, persuaded Schindler to shrug his shoulders and look with indifference on the extremities – cold nights, uncomfortably warm days, Santa Ana winds of the intensity of an oven, torrential rains, and days and weeks of clammy penetrating fog. Schindler's clients were willing to put up with this *laissez-faire* approach to climate in their summer and weekend houses, but not for long in houses where they dwelt all the year round. By the late twenties they had won him over, or at least had forced him to accept mechanical heating and cooling.

Though Schindler was determined to be his own man, he started his independent work of the early twenties by producing a series of designs which were close in spirit to Wright's and Lloyd Wright's designs of the same period. Historically these designs are closely related to the Expressionist phase of European architecture. Like the European Expressionists, the two Wrights and Schindler manipulated interlocking lines and volumes, rectangles and sharp angles to create a highly agitated composition. Part of the fascination of these motifs lies in their arbitrary quality. The fact that they have nothing to do, except by accident, with functional or constructional needs makes them

30   G. W. Smith Heberton house, Montecito, 1916

all the more intriguing. Since they are almost always realized as surface or surfaces, they establish a rich tactile quality, quite foreign to the rising International Style in Europe. The sources for Southern California's brief excursion into Expressionism are, as is generally the case with sources, anything but simple. Many of the motifs come from Wright himself – from his Midway Gardens of 1914 and from the Imperial Hotel in Tokyo, where he had at an early date shown an intense interest in the textile-patterned surfaces of Pre-Columbian architecture. We must not forget either that Schindler had a direct knowledge of current events in European Expressionist painting and architecture: at this time he kept closely abreast of what was going on, and in Los Angeles he, Kem Weber and Lloyd Wright knew Mrs Galka Scheyer and her collection of paintings by Klee, Kandinsky, Feininger and Jawlensky. The last of the possible sources for Schindler's Expressionism is the Zigzag Moderne, or Jazz Modern, which reached its climax in the 1925 Paris exhibition of Arts Décoratifs (hence the style's other name,

'Art Déco'). The similarity between many of the surface patterns used by the two Wrights and Schindler and the motifs of Zigzag Moderne is too close to be accidental. The new fashion was taken up with gusto in the Southland, and by the late *78* twenties all of the large architectural firms which were reshaping the business areas of Los Angeles had embraced it, while the Spanish Colonial Revival remained supreme in residential and *30* smaller business buildings.

While Schindler lampooned the Zigzag Moderne as a superficially applied style, many of his own surface patterns are different only in the motifs used – largely rectangular patterns rather than sharp angles, zigzags or curves. The small duplexes and houses which he designed for 'the speculative builder O. S. Floren in 1922–5 show how close Schindler came to being *49* fully committed to 'Jazz': the surface of these stucco boxes is decorated with rows of appliqué horizontal and vertical patterns.

More profoundly Expressionistic in feeling were his two schemes of 1923 for the unrealized house for Mrs Clode Warne at Los Angeles, and the final design for the C. P. Lowes house at Eagle Rock. The Warne house is an angled box, perched on *31* top of a wall. All four sides are composed of a busy pattern of overlaid boards, which press into and embrace a central panel of stucco and horizontal windows on the front, and a vertically articulated panel and grouping of windows and balconies on the side. The design is fascinating, but its fascination derives from the arbitrariness of the pattern. Like an ideal Palladian villa, it challenges us to guess how utilitarian needs can possibly be organized in such a piece of volumetric sculpture.

In the Lowes house, surfaces of linear overlapping boards *32* again act as a tactile foil to plain stuccoed surfaces; but here there is more complexity in the number of volumes which compose the whole. The slightly protruding bay of the south façade, and the den and upstairs sleeping porches on the west façade, are close in form to the surfaces of the Warne project. The three-level plan of the Lowes house logically responds to

31   First scheme for a house for Mrs Clode Warne, Los Angeles, 1923

32   House for C. P. Lowes, Eagle Rock, 1923

33   House for
C. P. Lowes,
Eagle Rock,
1923:
living room
fireplace

the south-sloping site and is oriented to give views of the valley
below. The space of the living room penetrates into the lower
dining room through an opening above the built-in buffet. High
clerestory windows on each side of the living room chimney   *33*
enhance the verticality of the main room. In the dining room
the major artificial light source is a fixture consisting of a vertically paired grouping of eight exposed light bulbs, which, with
their porcelain base, function as sculpture whether lit or unlit.

But while Schindler took great care with such details as
these light-fittings, and successfully related internal and external
space, he seems to have been more casual with other problems.
One enters directly from the outside into the living room,
without any transition; the front door seems almost an after-
thought – equally difficult to find from within and without. In
the Lowes house, as in so many of his designs, Schindler seems

57

to have been annoyed and impatient at having to provide stairs from one level to another. Considering that one of his prime concerns was the manipulation of vertical space (changes in ceiling and floor levels), it is surprising that he so rarely designed stairs that are a pleasure to use. In this house the stairs down to the dining area and up to the bedroom hall are both cramped in width and far too steep. Though the architect said that a kitchen should be designed to make cooking a pleasure, his kitchens are generally small and dingy. When larger, as in the Lowes house, they force the housewife to look at a blank wall as she does the dishes. Schindler wrote that the bath should be a spacious and pleasant exercise room, but in the Lowes house and elsewhere he produced baths that are minimal to the point of being cramped.

Equally Expressionist and quite as arbitrary in its exterior geometry, but far more successful functionally, is the John C. Packard house at South Pasadena (1924). Here Schindler developed further the theme of a complete man-made environment. As in the Kings Road house, the parents' room and the children's playroom are separate retreats; the sleeping spaces, including closets for the storage of clothes, are open porches extended off each retreat. The Y-shaped plan made it possible to lay out six exterior spaces – a service court, an entrance-living garden, a more secluded 'patio lawn', an enclosed 'glade', a playground and a garden off the parents' bedroom. Local restrictions required a gable roof: Schindler answered them, partly in irony, by covering the three arms of the house with high, sharply pitched roofs, punctured vertically by tall window bays. The interior space created by these high pitched roofs and their antithesis, low horizontal spaces, is the closest Schindler ever came to the spatial atmosphere of Bernard Maybeck. While the Y-shaped plan introduced a few awkward and un-resolved nooks and crannies, it was on the whole highly successful. The central kitchen opens directly to the service porch and entrance, and to the dining room: through double doors Mrs Packard could survey the children in the playroom. The

34, 35,
37

35

34

36, 37

58

34   House for John C. Packard, South Pasadena, 1924

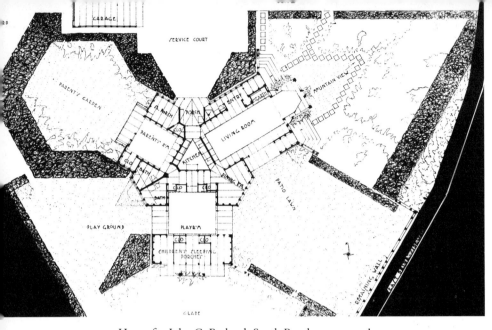

35 House for John C. Packard, South Pasadena, 1924: plan

37 House for John C. Packard, South Pasadena, 1924: living room ▶

36 BERNARD MAYBECK Hearst Hall, University of California, Berkeley, 1899

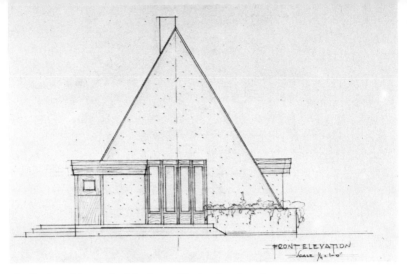

38　Projected house for Mrs Laura Davies, Los Angeles, *c.* 1922–4

injection of a central core provided a spatial and acoustic buffer between the several zones of the house, but at the same time the distance from one zone to the other was not great.

The Packard house was Schindler's first experience with gunnite concreting. The walls were composed of two separate layers of wire mesh which were tied to the vertical reinforcing rods of each of the interior posts; both the thin walls and the posts were gunnited (i.e. concrete was shot at them out of a gun) in one operation. This concrete system had several advantages over his previous tilt-slab technique: the air space in the wall provided a more effective barrier to moisture and to colder or warmer temperatures outside; the wall itself was thinner, and since it was much lighter than a solid slab of concrete, the foundations could be lighter. All the wooden elements of the Packard house – roofs, dormers, fascia, etc. – were to have been covered with thin sheets of copper, but the cost was too high, so instead Schindler used roll roofing, as he was to do later in other houses.

A year or two before the Packard house Schindler had designed another house with a high-pitched roof and almost no external walls. This was the small house for Mrs Laura *38* Davies in Los Angeles (*c.* 1922–4), which had an **A**-frame structure – one of the first in the United States. Another house with a dominant high-pitched roof, this time quite monumental in character, was to have been built in Hollywood for Mrs M. *39* Davis Baker (1923). While individual, these houses have much in common with Frank Lloyd Wright's concurrent work in Los Angeles. Schindler made no other experiments with sharply pitched roofs until the late thirties, when he used the A-frame again in the Bennati cabin (1934). He also returned to *97* the Maybeckian spatial atmosphere of the Packard house in one of his last houses, that for the Tischlers of 1949–50. *157*

39   Projected house for Mrs M. Davis Baker, Hollywood, 1923

Schindler's last essay in angular Expressionism was the Leah-Ruth Shop at Long Beach (1926). This was a remodelling, and he chose to place a screen of geometric pattern in front of the existing conventional shop front. This design smacks of the drawing board: it is two-dimensional, ignoring completely what lies behind. Its kinship is with the nineteenth-century false-fronted store, in which the entire front is an advertising sign. In his later store designs he also used the front as a 'come-on', but these fronts tend to be three-dimensional pieces of sculpture, rather than two-dimensional linear exercises.

40 IRVING GILL Dodge house, Hollywood, 1916

CHAPTER FIVE

Theories in practice

Schindler had seen a few of Irving Gill's buildings during his 1915 trip to the West Coast, but he and Neutra were really introduced through Lloyd Wright, who had worked for Gill in San Diego. Outwardly Schindler never responded very warmly to Gill's architecture: even though he had visited Gill in the early twenties and had the impressive Dodge house facing him across Kings Road, he was not willing to admit that there might be a similarity between Gill and his mentor Loos. Perhaps Gill's occasional use of the arch or of roof tiles carried too strong a suggestion of the Mission and Spanish Colonial Revivals for Schindler to appreciate the purity of his form. But he was quick to take up Gill's structural use of concrete, particularly the tilt-slab method. The one instance of a Schindler design which shows a close similarity to Gill is that for single and double concrete houses in a 'workmen's colony', for Gould and Bandini (1924). Both the site plan and the design of the individual buildings come very close to Gill's (and Frederick Law Olmstead Jr's) plan and housing for Torrance, of 1916. *41* Also it is reasonable to suppose that Gill's involvement with the popular bungalow court (especially his Lewis Courts, Sierra *42* Madre, 1910) encouraged Schindler in a similar direction. The projected bungalow court for Jacob Korsen in Los Angeles *43, 44* (1921) looks like a European's version of Gill's Horatio West Apartments at Santa Monica (1919); however the source of Schindler's design was not Gill, but his own 1912 thesis project. *5*

For California and really for the rest of the United States in the early twenties Schindler's Pueblo Ribera Court (later called *45–47* 'El Pueblo Ribera, the Indian Village') was one of the most original multiple housing designs of the period. From a planning point of view it was successful in almost every regard: in

41   IRVING GILL Workers' housing, Torrance, 1916

42   IRVING GILL Lewis Courts, Sierra Madre, 1910

43, 44   Projected bungalow court for Jacob Korsen, Los Angeles, 1921

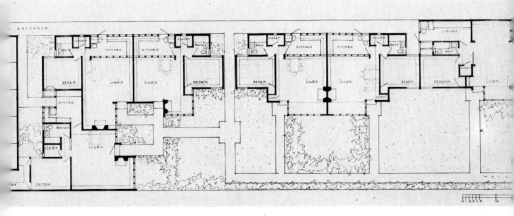

its streetscape, with its contrasts and contradictions, its coherence
45 and irregularity; in its provision for maximum privacy for
each unit; in its use of roof terraces so that each dwelling
enjoyed a view of the sea; and finally in its use of concrete
46 formed into walls by the use of movable forms. The dwellings
are treated as paired units forming an L. Each unit has its own
private outdoor room (patio), which is bounded by one
common blank wall and by high hedges. A second semi-
47 outdoor area is the roof terraces, which are for daytime living
and for sleeping at night. Sliding glass doors and paired French
doors open up the U-shaped interior space to the enclosed patio.
The Pueblo Ribera development, as its name implies, has something of the appearance of the Indian pueblo villages of New
Mexico. In detail it used the same low horizontal space and
159 contrast of wood and concrete as the Kings Road house; and
the way in which the horizontal windows are injected into the
layered concrete walls is structurally and visually identical to
18 that in the 1917 project for a log house.

The Pueblo Ribera scheme provides a visual case history of
the frustration that was involved for both client and architect
in realizing a modern building in the early twenties. Schindler's
client was W. L. Lloyd, a San Diego dentist. La Jolla had long
enjoyed a reputation as a beach resort, but it was in the late
teens and twenties that it experienced the most intensive building activity. Most of those who came to La Jolla were visitors
who sought to escape the rigours of the cold Middle Western
winters. What was needed in La Jolla was more rentable houses
and apartments, and Lloyd and others sought to cash in on the
demand. The client met Schindler through friends in Hollywood, late in 1922. He asked Schindler to create a complex
which would attract attention because of its design, but at the
same time would have a traditional Southwestern flavour. From
the point of view of the investor, who wanted maximum
utilization of his land, the bungalow court concept was the most
logical design to use. Schindler wrote to W. L. Lloyd in April
1923, 'I purpose to treat the whole in true California style – the

68

middle of the house being the garden, the rooms opening wide to it, the floors of concrete, close to the ground. The roof is to be used as a porch, either for living or sleeping.' Although Lloyd had wished for fourteen rather than twelve units, Schindler's plan for the land seemed economically sound to him.

The greatest problem at Pueblo Ribera was posed by the architect's insistence that the walls should be of concrete rather than wood frame. The client went to one lending agency after another, but they all baulked at the use of concrete. Their objection was that it would be more expensive, that there was no assurance that it would hold up, and that the low esteem in which concrete was held (good for basements and utilitarian structures, but not for the walls of houses) would make the units difficult to rent. Schindler assured his client that the new material would not cost any more and that 'a well-mixed concrete of proper proportions is in itself waterproof'. Lloyd finally raised the money by mortgaging himself to the hilt, and Schindler's friend Chase served as contractor for the building. 'Everyone here', wrote Lloyd, 'tells me concrete houses cannot be made water tight in the manner you have planned. I hope soon to be able to prove them in error.'

One horizontal layer was poured each day and then the frame was moved up to the next position. Reinforcing rods 46 were used both horizontally and vertically to tie the layers together. Floors, interior partitions and roof terraces, as well as door and window frames, were of untreated redwood.

The gloomy forecasts of the lending agencies proved to be altogether accurate. The concrete walls were more expensive (as they still are) than conventional wood studding. The agencies' doubts about how the concrete floors and walls would function were equally well grounded. Because the sand used in the mix was not well washed and the amount of cement used was minimum, the walls soon developed cracks and eventually the concrete began to flake off. The detailed design of the junction between wood and concrete was inadequate,

69

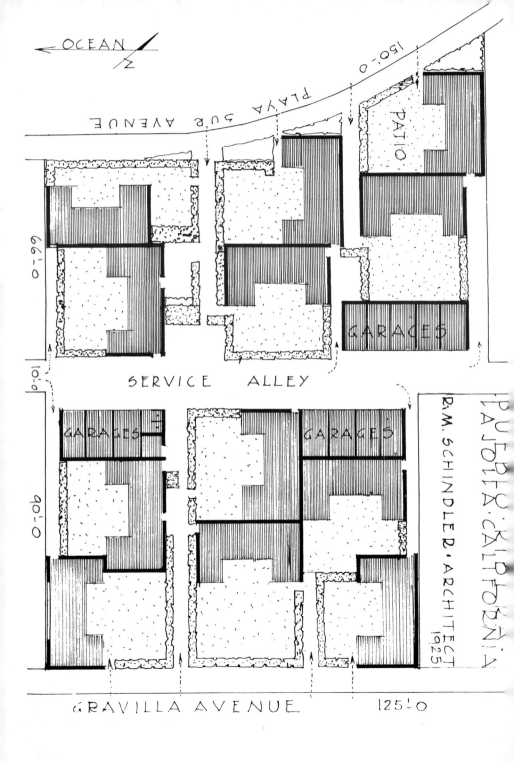

45–47 Pueblo Ribera Court, La Jolla, 1923: opposite, plan; above, construction of concrete walls; below, view along Playa Sur Avenue

and Schindler did not provide for proper drainage, because of his wish to keep the cost down. The result of all this was that the units leaked like a sieve. When it does rain in Southern California, during the winter, the amount which comes down in a limited time can be great (8 to 12 inches in 24 to 30 hours), and it goes without saying that a successful design should be expected to take such environmental factors into account. Lloyd wrote letter upon letter of distress to Schindler, vividly describing water pouring through roofs, running through doors and through cracks; tenants leaving in disgust, and so forth. Schindler and Chase improvised here and there and (by spending yet more money) remedied the worst of the evils, but the units were never completely water-tight. By the late twenties Lloyd was in such financial straits that he was forced to sell first one and then the other section of the court. As a land-use concept the Pueblo Ribera was admirable, but as an imposition of doctrinaire modern architecture on the real world of building and finance it was a failure.

48   A large-scale version of the Pueblo Ribera scheme was the housing project for J. Harriman, probably at Los Angeles (1924–5). Like the La Jolla scheme the Harriman project was an enlarged bungalow court treated as a self-contained community, with its own stores, gas (petrol) station – off the drawing to the right – garages, a playground and a community hall. Six rows of twenty-seven units were grouped on six terraces which stepped down to the river. Each rectangular unit contained a walled patio (the outdoor living room) and an enclosed L-shaped space which housed in its centre a living room with a dining nook; a kitchen and service porch made up one wing, the other containing the bedroom, dressing room and bath. Although supposedly oriented to the automobile (its entrance court, like that of the later motel, was an automobile entrance and twenty-one garages were provided), the Harriman housing demanded that some of the dwellers walk a whole city block to reach their unit. Nor was there any place allowed for guests and visitors to park. This project aptly reveals the difficulty of

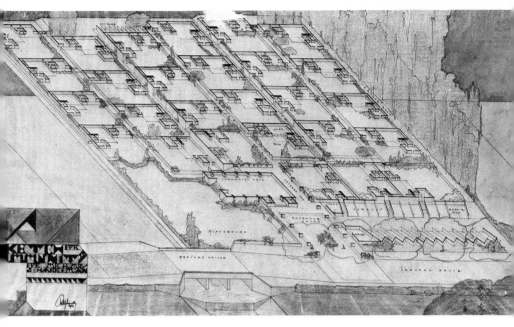

48   Housing project for J. Harriman, probably at Los Angeles, 1924-5

producing a horizontal development, based on the automobile,
without giving more ground space to access roads, parking and
garage space. If the automobile, as Schindler himself argued as
early as 1922, was to be the major mode of transportation, the
designer must work out his plan to bring it directly to the
front door of the dwelling. Schindler recognized this in placing
the garage and automobile entrance court immediately in front
of his community scheme, but then he did not solve the problem
of bringing the dweller to his abode. The Harriman project
was never built: whether this was due to the difficulties just
mentioned or to financing is not known.

From 1922 to 1925 Schindler worked closely with the
contractor-investor O. S. Floren. He produced a score or more
of designs for single-family houses, terrace houses and small *49*
apartments. His and Floren's aim was to build inexpensive

speculative housing which could compete with the popular housing being put up by other contractors. In this they succeeded. The costs were kept down by using conventional building techniques (the stucco-covered wood frame) and by keeping designs extremely simple in their surfaces and volumes. Outwardly these buildings, with their superimposed rows of horizontal and vertical raised lines and monolithic Pre-Columbian appearance, were certainly more Zigzag Moderne than modern.

Somewhat different from these Pre-Columbian designs were his project for an eight-unit apartment building for Floren at Los Angeles (1924) and his apartment building for S. Breacher, also at Los Angeles (1925). Both in massing and detail the Breacher apartments sway between the Zigzag Moderne and the International Style; the volumes appear heavy (in Schindler's own term, 'sculptured-architecture'), while the balance and the symmetry of the plan seems traditional and classical. The corner windows, with their horizontal mullions, have the flavour of styling rather than of something integral to the scheme. Designs in a similar vein came off Schindler's drawing board during his association with Neutra and Arnovici in the Architectural Group for Industry and Commerce. Their four-storey Garden Apartments in Hollywood (finally completed by Neutra in 1927) and their project for an auditorium and civic centre for Richmond (1930) were also both Moderne and modern.

50

49   Double house designed for O. S. Floren, Hollywood, 1923

50　Apartment building for S. Breacher, Los Angeles, 1925

Less Moderne, but still displaying superimposed lines – this time of narrow vertical boards connected to roof outriggers – were his Sachs apartments at Los Angeles (1926–40). On a steep hillside site lying between two streets, he placed the units as a series of steps which descend the slope. The larger apartments back on to the upper street and open out on to small roof garden balconies. The smaller apartments on the lower street are above street-level garages. A stepped public walkway, with Schindler's impossible steps, penetrates through the site and through the buildings, leading from one street to the other. As with his designs for Floren, the structure was a stucco-covered wooden balloon frame. The outward forms of the Sachs are more self-consciously abstract than any of his earlier apartment designs. While some of his interpenetration of forms was achieved through volumes, most of it was through changes in surface pattern – the shape and pattern of window openings, of wood surface, of applied vertical batten boards, all contrasting with the plain stucco surfaces. Close up, these contrasts are far too busy and rich, but seen from a distance the basic stepped volumes are impressive as a small, low density complex.

51

CHAPTER SIX

The making of a personal style

The finest of Schindler's designs of the 1920s are those which could loosely be labelled de Stijl. With the one exception that he never relied on primary colours to establish or reinforce forms (he seems almost to have been frightened by colour), this body of Schindler's work is closely parallel to the designs of the Dutch de Stijl architects of the early twenties, especially Theo van Doesburg, and to a lesser extent Gerrit Rietveld and Mart Stam. Van Doesburg's careful sculptural arrangements of volumes and of horizontal planes, which penetrate and con- 52 nect the separate volumes, is in many ways similar to Schindler's. The Constructivist element in Rietveld's designs appears in several of Schindler's designs, particularly in his Lovell beach house of 1922–6. It was during the early twenties that Schindler began to develop what was to become his personal architectural idiom. Certain of his design concepts can easily be accounted for in his Viennese experience and in his simplification of the Wright mode; but these two factors can explain only partially the strong de Stijl flavour.

Schindler could never have developed as he did without an acute awareness of what was going on in avant-garde European architectural circles during the twenties. That he had such a close knowledge is shown by his personal file of cuttings which contain pages from a good number of the major European architectural journals, including *Die Bau Gilde, Moderne Bauformen, Soziale Bauwirtschaft, L'Amour de l'art, Das Werk* and *International Studio*. Here can be found designs by van Doesburg, Oud, Rietveld, Le Corbusier, Gropius and Mendelsohn. These cuttings were all filed alphabetically by the architect's name and in some instances by building type; and the collection was added to continually right up until the time of his death. There

◀ 51 Manola Court, apartment building for H. Sachs, Los Angeles, 1926–40

can be no question that he knew what was going on, and that he knew in what ways his work did or did not fit into Expressionism and the later International Style, or for that matter into Zigzag Moderne and the later Streamlined.

A look at his buildings of the early and mid-twenties shows how he sloughed off the more fidgety of Wright's design elements and worked increasingly with a vocabulary of volumes. He desired that his building as an object in space should be a Neo-Plastic piece of sculpture, and that internally a similar Neo-Plastic vocabulary should be used to create his horizontal and vertical Loosian space. A turning point in divesting himself of Wright was the house for James E. Howe in Los Angeles (1925). The Howe and the later C. H. Wolfe house at Avalon (1928) were his works most frequently illustrated during this decade. In the Howe house vertical walls, horizontal roof planes and secondary volumes radiate from a central cube.

53, 54
74, 75

53, 54   House for J. E. Howe, Los Angeles, 1925; above, view towards the kitchen
and living room (from bottom left in plans); below, plans

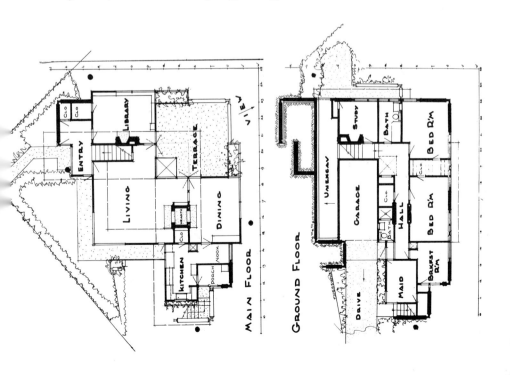

Slip-form concrete walls visibly attach the structure tightly to its hillside site. The use of horizontal boards of redwood, with their joints covered by battens, is the only strongly Wrightian feature still remaining. The continuation of the horizontal battens through the main window units as transoms (a device Wright was to use frequently during the thirties) implied that the walls and glass areas were paper-thin surfaces entirely lacking in mass.

The two works of the twenties which most interested architects and critics in the fifties and sixties are Schindler's Kings Road house, and his house for Dr Phillip Lovell at Newport Beach (1922–6). The former received a few minor notices in the architectural press during the interwar years; the latter was *55–57,* all but ignored. Today the Lovell beach house deserves a place *59–61,* with Neutra's Lovell house (1929), Gropius' Bauhaus at Dessau *58* (1925–6), Le Corbusier's Villa Savoye at Poissy (1929–30) and Mies van der Rohe's German Pavilion at Barcelona (1929) as a key work of twentieth-century architecture. While it cannot match them as an art object, it does equal them as a doctrinaire assertion of the new architecture. Even with (or perhaps because of) its inconsistencies and unresolved parts, the Lovell beach house is the only one of these five buildings which comes anywhere near to fulfilling the ideals of the International Style as set forth in 1932 by Henry-Russell Hitchcock and Philip Johnson, in their exhibition at the newly organized Museum of Modern Art in New York – though, ironically, the Lovell house was the only one not included in the exhibition. Hitchcock and Johnson established in the chapter headings of their catalogue three 'principles' which underlay the New Style: 'Architecture as Volume'; 'Concerning Regularity'; and 'The Avoidance of Applied Decoration'. The Lovell beach house perfectly subscribes to these three principles. Its enclosed space 'is no longer the dense brick, but the open box' (how closely this echoes Schindler's 1912 Manifesto). Its structure and enclosing walls are dramatically separated though, in contrast to Internationalist dogma, Schindler places his supports outside,

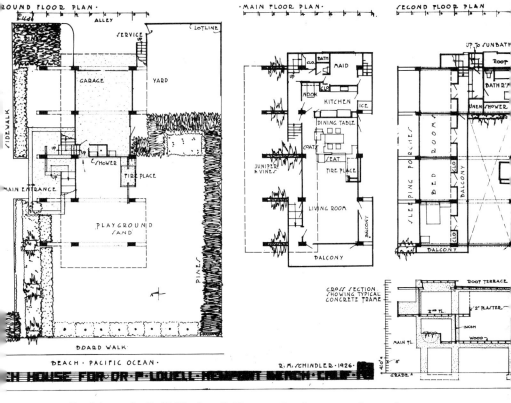

GROUND FLOOR PLAN·   ·MAIN FLOOR PLAN·   SECOND FLOOR PLAN

ALLEY

SERVICE

LOTLINE

GARAGE   YARD

SIDEWALK

SHOWER

MAIN ENTRANCE

FIRE PLACE

PLAYGROUND
SAND

PINES

BOARD WALK

BEACH · PACIFIC OCEAN·

R. M. SCHINDLER · 1926·

UP TO SUNBATH

CLO. BATH   MAID

NOOK   KITCHEN

ICE.

DINING TABLE

COAT   SEAT

JUNIPER
& VINES

FIRE PLACE

SLEEPING PORCHES   BED ROOM   BALCONY

ROOF

BATH R'M

LINEN SHOWER

CLO.

LIVING ROOM

BALCONY   CLO.

BALCONY

DALCONY

CROSS SECTION·
SHOWING TYPICAL
CONCRETE FRAME

ROOF TERRACE

2" PLASTER·

SASH

WOOD·

8"

MAIN FL.

GRADE·

55, 56   Beach house for Dr Phillip Lovell, Newport Beach, 1925–6: above, plans;
below, the house under construction

rather than inside, the building. The walls become, as Hitchcock and Johnson insisted, 'merely planes surrounding a volume'. The de Stijl composition of surfaces and volumes, particularly

59 at the rear of the house and inside, certainly expresses an awareness that 'the essence of architecture lies in the relation of the various sorts of geometrical projections', so that 'the more consistently a surface is arranged, the more conspicuous will be its character as a surface'. As to its plan, the open two-storey

61 space of the beach house emphasizes 'the unity and continuity of the whole volume inside of the building'. Yet Johnson was logical when he wrote that the house could not be included in the 1932 exhibition because it did not reflect the International Style as style.

Dr Phillip Lovell and his wife enjoy the rare distinction of having commissioned two of the major monuments of the Modern Movement – the beach house by Schindler and later a

58 house by Neutra. Dr Lovell was a characteristic Southern California product. It is doubtful whether his career could have been repeated anywhere else. Through his *Los Angeles Times*

57 Beach house for Dr Phillip Lovell, Newport Beach, 1925–6: detail of façade

column 'Care of the Body' (as we have seen), and through 'Dr Lovell's Physical Culture Center' he had an influence which extended far beyond the physical care of the body. He was, and he wished to be considered, progressive, whether in physical culture, permissive education or architecture. Like the newly emerging Hollywood stars of the twenties, his whole life was public. His home life, or at least the image of it, broadcast his message as much as his writings and professional life: his house therefore had to be an expression of how he wished himself to be seen. Not only should it directly demonstrate the high priority he placed on function; it should be wrapped in a scintillatingly novel package – and he had the funds to purchase it. Dr Lovell was thus the ideal client for the evangelistic modern architect who wished to experiment with form, but who likewise was involved in the morality of fitness to purpose.

Life in the open was to be the theme of the beach house: it was to be an argument (repeated in the Neutra design) for health and modernity combined. The house was placed on 57, 59 stilts, not only to provide some privacy from the public beach and to obtain a view of the ocean, but so that the beach could penetrate under the house, forming an outdoor sheltered living space equipped with its own fireplace. In a beach house, Schindler had even more reason than in a normal town house to omit bedrooms, providing only personal, enclosed dressing rooms adjoining an open sleeping porch. Physical exercise and sun bathing could be carried out (in private) in the open shelter on the roof of the house. The rest of the building 60, 61 (exclusive of bath and kitchen) was one large informal room to be used by the entire family.

In discussing the five concrete frames which lift the house above the beach, Schindler wrote, 'The motif used in elevating the house was suggested by the pile structure indigenous to all beaches.' He looked at the enclosed space as something independent of the frames. 'All walls and partitions are two inches thick. They are made of metal lath and cement plaster, suspended between the concrete frames.' The architect and

60 Beach house for Dr Phillip Lovell, Newport Beach, 1925–6: living room ▶

the client first discussed the beach house in the fall of 1922. Schindler's one surviving sketch of that year shows that the basic form of the house was decided on at that time. He had toyed with and abandoned several alternative methods of supporting his roof within the five concrete frames, including one scheme with a central mast and radiating diagonal wires.

The beach house as constructed beautifully illustrates Robert Venturi's concept of great architecture: '. . . I like elements which are . . . inconsistent and equivocal rather than direct and clear. I am for messy vitality over obvious unity.' The strong assertiveness of the concrete forms is countered by the assertive nature of the independent existence of the volumes. The clean, smooth machine surfaces do battle with small passages of agitated Wrightian details. Significantly it was these Wrightian details, especially in the patterned window mullions, which upset the exponents and propagandists of the International Style.

The strong Constructivist element which underlay the design of the Lovell beach house was never again completely exploited by Schindler. There are a few later instances, such as the exposure of the frame and its diagonal bracing in the projected Physical Education Club Lodge for Topanga Ranch (Topanga Canyon, Los Angeles County, 1923), but there were no examples of Constructivism after 1925.

As Esther McCoy has pointed out, the cheapness, ease of insulation and dryness of American wood frame construction was such that few if any clients were willing to – or could afford to – use either steel or concrete for domestic construction. Schindler's almost exclusive use of the stucco-covered wood frame from the mid-twenties was, of course, not only a response to economics. The change was also aesthetic: his interest from then on was almost exclusively in the play of thin rectangular volumes, expressed in non-monumental sculptural terms. After half a dozen years in California he had reached the decision that the thing to do was not to fight existing building technology, but to accept it and to use it for his own end;

61   Beach house for Dr Phillip Lovell, Newport Beach, 1925–6: living room ▶

and his end still remained that of the artist-architect – the manipulation of form. But now he would use the everyday means of low art (the technology of the run-of-the-mill contractor) to realize his high art ideals. In taking over builders' techniques, he ended up by taking over much more, as he seems to have sensed almost immediately. His buildings, like those of contractors, became unsubstantial, thin and cardboardy; and this quality, which distressed the critics of the time, rapidly became an integral part of his visual language. He was no longer interested in establishing all or even a fraction of his form through structural expressionism. It has even been suggested, by Esther McCoy, that the fragile, fleeting and impermanent came to appeal to Schindler as 'a kind of protest against the Establishment'. This may have been subconsciously true, but the fine realization of stucco-covered wood construction in the later Buck and Rodakiewicz houses, where adequate budgets were provided, indicates that he had embraced the impermanent not as a protest, but rather as a means of realizing his forms. If his client's budget were restricted and limited (as it usually was), he would pare the structure to the bone so that he could obtain the formal and spatial aspects he was seeking. Except for a few instances in the thirties, he abandoned his image as architect-engineer for that of artist-architect.

99–100,
127–129

As his practice developed in the twenties it became increasingly apparent to Schindler that while he was maturing as a designer, he was hardly making a success at the business of architecture. He could, and very often did, kindle deep and lasting enthusiasm in his clients (especially in his female clients), but he had little or no contact with the business world of Los Angeles. His commercial work was limited to a few store remodellings. Unlike other figures of the Modern Movement, Schindler was seldom interested in producing a design for its own sake, to solve some hypothetical problem: he liked to work with actual situations, even if the chances of building were marginal.

Like Mies van der Rohe, Mart Stam and Walter Gropius,

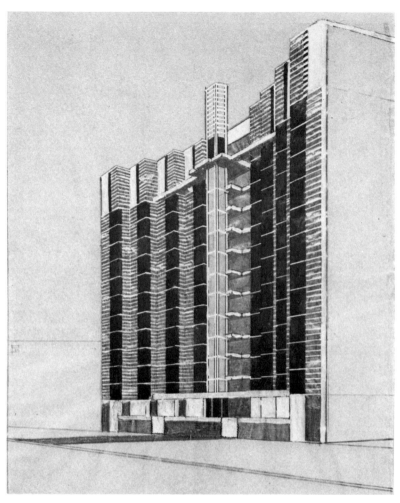

62 Project for The Playmart, skyscraper of black glass and aluminium, Los Angeles, 1921

Schindler tackled the problem of the high-rise building early in his career. His project for a twelve-storey Playmart sky-scraper in Los Angeles, of black glass and aluminium (1921), 62 is a wonderful mixture of Constructivism, de Stijl and Moderne, with a strong touch of Southern Californian exhibitionism. If Mies' sharp angular glass skyscraper of 1921–2 can be spoken

of as Expressionist, then Schindler's is super-Expressionist. Its street façade steps in on both sides, centring on an open glazed elevator tower, which stands separate within the building, connected to each floor by bridges. The neutral steel cage of the building is openly acknowledged, but the appliqué pattern of alternating black glass and aluminium bands visually establishes the horizontal as the dominant note. He used black glass and aluminium, with their Moderne implications, only once more in the twenties: this was for the projected Peoples
63   Bank in Los Angeles (1924).

Schindler's final attempt to be the architect-engineer-businessman was prompted by Neutra's arrival in California in 1925. Immediately after Neutra came (he and his wife lived for several years with the Schindlers at the Kings Road house), the two Viennese architects began to collaborate on projects. In the earliest of these joint efforts Neutra landscaped several

63   Project for The Peoples Bank, Los Angeles, 1924

houses which Schindler had already designed: the garden schemes for both the Howe house and the Lovell beach house 53–55 were by Neutra. The relationship between Schindler and Neutra varied considerably from project to project. Since the designing took place in Schindler's studio house, it would be reasonable to suppose that in such daily contact the two men affected each other's work. It would not be unreasonable to suggest that Neutra's presence was one of the major forces which encouraged Schindler to rid himself of his bag of fussy Wrightian details which he still used on occasion. The cleaned-up machine-like quality of Schindler's buildings of the thirties, his increased use of hard, non-tactile materials, and his rejection of 'warm' materials, especially wood, during much of his de Stijl phase of the thirties probably owed much to the stimulus of Neutra.

Between 1926 and 1931 the cooperative ventures of Schindler and Neutra – joined by the urban planner Carol Arnovici – carried the signature of the Architectural Group for Industry and Commerce (AGIC). The AGIC concentrated their efforts on larger commercial and governmental buildings. These ranged from an 'amusement centre' to cafés, hotels, and apartment houses. Their largest planning schemes were for the Falcon Flyers Country Club, near Wasco (undated, c. 1927–8), the auditorium and civic centre at Richmond (1930), and a series of 'highway bungalow hotels' (no locations given, signed only by Schindler and Arnovici, 1931). Not one was built.

Why such a poor record? The answer probably lies not in the economic unfeasibility of their designs nor in the fact that they were modern, but in the character and marginal financial backing of their clients. The Richmond project was begun, but had to be abandoned eventually because of the economic conditions of the depression. If the larger businesses and corporations of Los Angeles wished to have a building packaged in the Moderne mode, this, like other commodities, could be ordered with confidence from one of the large well-established architectural firms; there was no reason or advantage in going to way-out 'artists' for this sort of product.

In addition to the AGIC, Schindler and Neutra jointly sub-64–66 mitted a design to the League of Nations Competition in 1926, which has remained virtually unknown up to the present day. From the very beginning it was eclipsed by Le Corbusier's impressive design and the superb public relations which have always surrounded that entry. Yet the two schemes have many points in common: both are dually oriented to land and water transportation (and in the case of the Schindler-Neutra project, air transportation by sea-plane); both emphasize the separation of the courtrooms, assembly chambers, and the office space for the secretariat and for the commissions. In the Schindler-Neutra design the secretariat is treated as a single rectangular office block while the slanted floor of the seating space of the 66 assembly chambers is reflected externally. The Schindler-Neutra project, like the Lovell beach house, is far more Constructivist than Le Corbusier's design. The enclosed volume of the secretariat is suspended below a series of U-shaped concrete frames, in contrast to the box-on-stilts which Le Corbusier used.

The question of who contributed what to the joint project will probably never be answered to full satisfaction. The idea of entering an international competition has more the ring of Neutra than of Schindler; but although at the time of its submission it was officially listed as by Neutra and Schindler, local publicity about the project in Los Angeles has always mentioned Schindler's name first. The final presentation drawings are by Neutra, but many of the preliminary studies are by Schindler. The block layout of the scheme and also the detailing of the secretariat building suggest Neutra rather than Schindler; but 65 the assembly hall, with its stepped floors cantilevered out over the lake and its inventive manner of introducing natural and artificial light (through slanted roof windows which are not visible from within the auditorium), should probably be credited to Schindler. It is reasonable, therefore, to look at the

94

64, 65   SCHINDLER AND RICHARD J. NEUTRA Project for the League of Nations
Building, 1926: above, perspective drawing; below, elevation of assembly hall

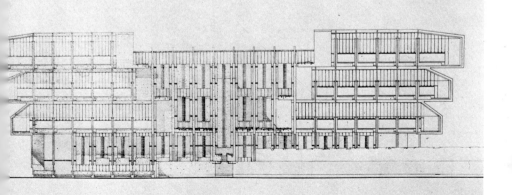

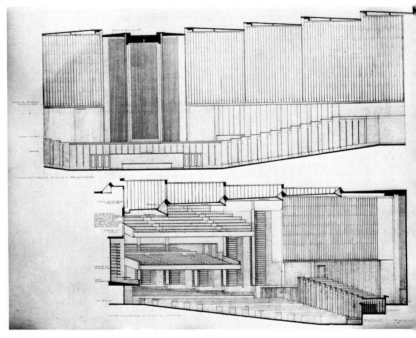

66 SCHINDLER AND RICHARD J. NEUTRA Project for the League of Nations Building, 1926: section of auditorium

design as a joint project; something which neither designer could have achieved independently.

In view of the long-term publicity which Le Corbusier received from his project for the League, it is strange that the only notable American entry was shunned by both the American and European press; even though Neutra had a sophisticated appreciation of the need for publicity. The Schindler-Neutra drawings were shown along with Le Corbusier's in a travelling exhibition in France and Germany and they received a brief mention in American newspapers – that was all. Possibly the fact that it was a joint production discouraged both men from pressing it for what it was worth.

The day-to-day operation of the Architectural Group for Industry and Commerce must have been a strange hybrid from the very beginning, the sole connecting link being a shared evangelism for the new. Of the three, Arnovici could collaborate with the most profit to himself, since his interest was in the theory of planning, not in the act of putting pencil to paper; but each of the two architects was a 'loner', both as a designer and as a personality. Yet in the end both did profit from the experience. Schindler's work was cleaned up and became more convincingly symbolic of the machine: to see this, one need only place his 1929 AGIC project for a hotel alongside his 67 1921 design for a skyscraper of black glass and aluminium. The 62 complex interrelation of numerous small volumes has been reduced to a few overriding forms. Only the conscious expression of the structure differentiates Schindler's later work from that of Neutra or some of the European Internationalists.

67   Project for a hotel, Hollywood, 1929

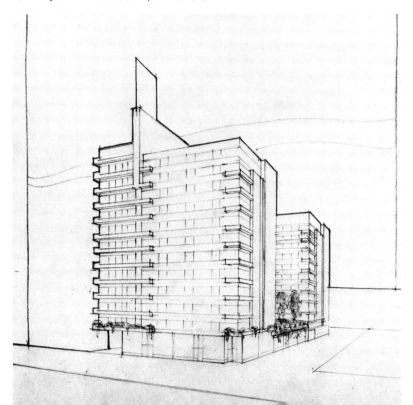

For Neutra the AGIC provided a desirable introduction to the American scene, and from a business point of view it enabled him to set up his own independent Los Angeles practice, for through his association with the AGIC he obtained his first large commissions – a garden apartment building in Los Angeles (1927) and the town house for the Lovells, also in Los Angeles (1929). The designs for these two buildings, particularly for the Lovell house, and his adroit handling of their publicity, established Neutra's reputation both in Europe and in the United States. By 1930, Neutra's name began to be mentioned with those of Gropius and Le Corbusier, while Schindler remained as a minor and, in certain ways, perverse architectural figure.

Even in the area where one would have thought that Schindler's designs would have been sure of success, the retail

68   Braxton Gallery, Hollywood, 1928

store, he was overshadowed in popularity by other Los Angeles designers – J.R. Davidson, Jacques Peters and Kem Weber. *78* These three designer-architects, all of whom were close friends of Schindler, were successful in projecting the new image of the industrial designer; whereas Schindler's image remained that of the artist-architect in his garret; even though his store designs proclaimed machine-made modernity to as great a degree as those of the others. In the narrow interior space of his small Braxton Gallery in Los Angeles (1928), Schindler used a *68* pattern of angled and stepped walls, showcases and desks to draw the customer through the store and into the main gallery at the rear. The tiny street façade asserted the machine in a *69* theatrical fashion through an ingenious movable steel and canvas awning (to keep the western sun out of the shop). The sheets of angled glass, the pattern of the upper steel supports, the bands of dark blue canvas and the vertical polished letters at the end of the awning superbly transformed the front into a single advertising sign.

Schindler's typographical and furniture designs of the twenties were similarly varied in their exploration of design ideas. His layout for posters, signs, advertisements and letter-heads was simply that of his architectural forms flattened out in two dimensions; while his furniture was, in its essence, *28, 61,* miniature architecture. His Viennese lettering style remained *74* fixed, even though he once or twice experimented with Wrightian jigsaw puzzles, as in the lettering for the Harriman Community Project of 1924. It was not until the late twenties *48* that he began to use letter faces which were similar in style to those popularized by the Bauhaus and the Internationalists.

As an inheritance from the turn-of-the-century Arts and Crafts movement, Schindler wished to have total control over all details within his buildings. Like both the Prairie architects and the Internationalists, he firmly believed in building-in as much furniture as possible. The image of the ship's cabin, which came to epitomize the modern, as well as the Streamlined Moderne, of the thirties, was also his ideal; his interiors can

70   Remodelled bathroom for Aline Barnsdall, Olive Hill, Los Angeles, 1925

◀ 69   Braxton Gallery, Hollywood, 1928

aptly be labelled 'cabinate architecture'. His first furniture was like Wright's, but scaled down and more comfortable, while his early chairs and tables of redwood are as Constructivist as his architecture. His built-in furniture, for instance in the Lovell beach house, is as much a de Stijl composition as the house 60 itself; but at the same time the sofa is comfortable and the adjoining shelves useful. The electric light as a sculptural element continually fascinated him; for the Lovell beach house he produced a floor lamp which was a vertical column of alternating wood and exposed light bulbs. In the corner of the living room 61 was a built-in vertical band of exposed light bulbs which repeated the mullion patterns of the great window.

By 1926, following a course already set by Breuer, Stam, Le Corbusier and Mies, he was designing steel furniture along with his Los Angeles colleagues, Weber, Davidson and Peters. As pieces of machine sculpture, and equally as comfortable seats, 68 his bent tubular steel chairs for the Braxton Gallery are notable, though they do not bear comparison with those designed by the European Internationalists.

Throughout the twenties, Aline Barnsdall remained a continual client for Schindler. At first with Lloyd Wright (who was trained as a landscape architect) and later alone, he projected various landscape schemes for Olive Hill; but almost all of these remained on paper. He did design and see built a wading pool and adjoining pergola (1925), and he designed a temporary outdoor exhibition space for paintings. Most of the time, to satisfy Aline Barnsdall's restless spirit, he was kept busy remodelling one or another of her three houses on Olive Hill. 70 His remodelling in 1925 of the main bathroom of Oleanders represents one of the rare occasions in which he used colour rather than volumes to establish his design. In a fashion highly reminiscent of the recent work of Charles Moore, the vertical row of coloured bands purposely denies the differentiation of surfaces and volumes (i.e. the architecture itself); the floor, the side of the tub, the tub shelf and the adjacent wall are tied together so that the separate quality of each is denied.

102

Before Schindler settled on his de Stijl mode of the late twenties and thirties he did one radically different design which lies outside this framework. In 1927, even though she had long since abandoned Hollyhock House for the smaller residence, 'B', Aline Barnsdall decided that she had had enough of the monument on Olive Hill and that she would build a secluded retreat along the upper coast of the Palos Verdes Peninsula. By now Schindler was fully conscious of the different micro-climates of Southern California. The Palos Verdes area enjoys a year-round cool climate (around 60–75 °F); often it is en-shrouded by fog and mist, and the winds from the ocean can be strong, continual and cold. The two elements needed to counter the adverse features of the climate are seclusion from

71

71   Projected Translucent House for Aline Barnsdall, Palos Verdes, 1927

the winds and the introduction of a maximum amount of light into the interior. Schindler easily solved the first problem by orienting the U-shaped courtyard so that its back was to the prevailing winds, and then by introducing sheltered spaces protected by partial walls and roofs. His solution to the light problem was to clothe the upper zone of the battened walls of the house with translucent glass (hence the name 'Translucent House'), panels of which fold over and form the first eighteen inches of the flat roof. Within, the impression is of a horizontal roof plane floating over a glass area. While the metal, glass and wood walls and the roof units were extremely advanced in design, the working drawings indicate that the house could nevertheless easily have been built with existing technology.

CHAPTER SEVEN

Schindler's 'de Stijl'

The year 1928 marks Schindler's full commitment to de Stijl. As already suggested, to apply the term 'de Stijl' to his work is only partially appropriate, in that it suggests his designs were wholly or to a large degree derived from the original Dutch de Stijl experiments of van Doesburg and others. They do have one essential point in common with European de Stijl (and here the term includes not only the Dutch originators, but other figures such as Frederick Kiesler): the use of intersecting rather than singular volumes to establish their forms. This feature is what most strongly differentiates Schindler's work from that of the closely knit Internationalists – Gropius, Mies, Le Corbusier (pre-1935) and Neutra.

Schindler's de Stijl repertory comprises a limited array of motifs which he repeats again and again, on scales ranging from large wall units to small details and furniture. The most frequently used is the open-key pattern: ⌐. These keys interlock with each other and project out of or into other surfaces or volumes, working both as sculpture and as a meaningful utilitarian aspect of the buildings. Other motifs which he frequently uses are the low-stemmed L, flattened Z, and rectangular planes which partially overlay one another. In contrast to much of his work of the twenties, he detaches the buildings visually from their sites. But his de Stijl motifs were used principally as a means to establish his own highly personal space – a space which had little to do with the horizontal layer-cake of the classic Internationalist.

In the last of his houses of the twenties – the Grokowsky *72–77* house at South Pasadena (1928), the Wolfe house at Avalon (1928), the projected Diffen house at Avalon (1929) and the projected Braxton house at Venice, California (1928–30) – he

divorces the building from its site. The small Grokowsky house
72, balances gently above the trees and shrubs of its landscapes;
76, 77 the Braxton house is a precise man-made form set down on a
73–75 beach; and the hillside houses for Wolfe and Diffen carry the
dissociation between site and man-made object to a dramatic
level. The Wolfe house was, as Schindler wrote, 'a composition
of space units to float above the hill': his description of it as a
form suspended over, but not connected to, the hillside indicates
that he was embracing one more doctrine of the Internationalists and abandoning another Wrightian concept.

The stepped four-tiered Wolfe house was designed with a
flexible arrangement of interior space, so that the house could
be used as a single-family unit or as a two- or three-family unit.
While the roof terrace was connected directly to the main
75 third level, the lower two floors were entirely independent. As
Loos would have arranged, the sleeping space on the main
74 floor was raised four feet above the living room, and was connected to it by means of three ascending volumes which
served both as steps and as seats. The wall-to-wall carpet of the
sleeping level wrapped over the edge of it and continued six
inches down the wall, thus tying the two areas together in an
even more effective fashion. The two elevations, to the road
and to the harbour, are so unlike that they might belong to
two different buildings. The harbour side relies on volumes
and on horizontal extensions from the volumes; while on the
road side the wood screen, the thin wood ramp and the vertical
struts of the roof terrace are completely linear. The inde-
pendence and conscious contrast of two or more elevations
89, 90 becomes even more pronounced an ambiguity in Schindler's
work of the thirties.

The Braxton house on the Venice beach was to be a rect-
76, 77 angular box into and out of which secondary volumes projected. Like the Lovell house, the main floor is one level above
ground, but this was not emphasized visually. The entire site is
treated as controlled and usable space – a garage and forecourt
toward the street, a covered walk and an open but walled patio,

106

72   House for D. Grokowsky, South Pasadena, 1928

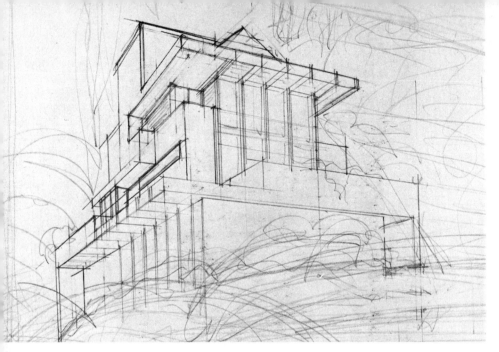

73   Projected remodelling of house for H. D. Diffen, Avalon, Catalina Island, 1929

74, 75   Summer house for C. H. Wolfe, Avalon, Catalina Island, 1928: below,
view from living room to bedroom; opposite, exterior

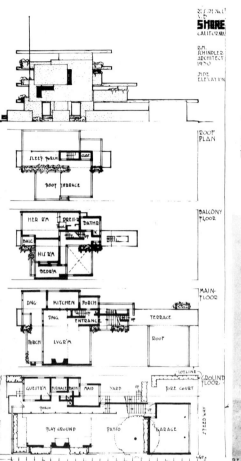

76, 77   Projected house for H. Braxton, Venice, 1928–30 (as drawn up in 1930 for V.B. Shore): left, elevation and plans; below, view from the beach, at left in the plan

77   and a unified playground with projecting rooms. The cube which forms the living room penetrates upwards into the third level. While a sleeping porch and a terrace are perched on top of the house, conventional bedrooms on the third level now face out over the ocean front. Even the dining porch is now partially walled and glazed as a response to the cool ocean winds. The Braxton house design shows that the architect was slowly giving up his *laissez-faire* view of Southern California and its climate, and was demanding an increased control over nature.

CHAPTER EIGHT

The depression: a new clientèle

The stock market crash of 1929, and the depression which followed it, dealt Southern California a severe blow. The narrowness of its economy made the region excessively sensitive to any boom or bust. By 1934, 300,000 people were unemployed in Los Angeles alone, and these were joined by an influx of destitute and uprooted Midwestern farmers and workers. The only extensive industry, oil, was particularly hard hit. Tourism, which had always been so important (in fact and in myth), slowed to a trickle. Thus began a decade's experiments with radical politics, ranging from leftish liberalism to communism. Upton Sinclair, with his mildly socialistic Epic programme, narrowly failed to be elected Governor of California in 1934. Other socialistic movements were initiated: for a brief moment Technocracy enjoyed a following (1932–5); this was followed by the most popular of all, the Townsend Plan (founded in 1934), which offered a universal 'Old Age Revolving Pension'. The last great radical assertion was the 'Ham and Eggs' proposal, which California almost adopted in 1938 with a vote of 1,143,000 in favour and 1,398,000 opposed. Like the tip of an iceberg, this expression of radicalism in California in the thirties scarcely conveyed the intensity of public disillusion with the twenties image of *laissez-faire* exploitation.

The one economic bright spot on the Southern California scene was the motion picture industry, which not only withstood the crash, but actually benefited from the bleakness of the depression years – for the Hollywood films provided *the* obtainable dream world for millions during the grim years of the thirties. As Carey McWilliams pointed out in *Southern California Country* (1946), 'If ever an industry played the Fairy Prince to an impoverished Cinderella, it has been the motion picture industry in relation to Los Angeles.'

What sort of men and women emerged in the thirties as the clients of the new architecture? As a group, they were liberal to lukewarm radicals in their politics and social outlook, Democrats almost to a man, and intensely anti-Republican. Many of them were directly or at least indirectly associated with the motion picture industry; others were book dealers, lawyers, professors and teachers.

In architecture, the early thirties marked a major turning point for the United States and, above all, for California. By 1929–30 all of the major architectural firms in Los Angeles were working in the language of the Zigzag Moderne. The crowning jewel of downtown Los Angeles was the shimmering black-and-gold Richfield Building (by Morgan, Walls and Clements, 1928), which was without doubt the best of the American black-and-gold skyscrapers. Vertical 'Zigzag' buildings were erected up and down the entire length of Wilshire Boulevard: the Bullock-Wilshire Store (by John and Donald Parkinson, with interiors by Jacques Peters, 1928) was as slickly fashionable as any Zigzag Moderne building in New York or Paris.

78

The Southern California practitioners of the Zigzag Moderne, like their compatriots elsewhere, saw architecture for what it was – primarily packaging. In this sense they were realists who saw what their own world was all about. What they failed to notice was that the initiative to establish and manipulate fashion was (by 1930) no longer really theirs. The proponents of high art architecture were being hard pressed; the founders of the new fashions of the thirties were the low art industrial designers. A symbolic union between industry and art occurred in the closing years of the twenties, all the major American designers emerging at this time: Walter Dorwin Teague in 1926, Norman Bel Geddes in 1927, Raymond Loewy in 1929, and Henry Dreyfus in 1929. These New York-based designers were joined by four Californians: Kem Weber, J.R. Davidson, Paul T. Frankl and Jacques Peters. Frankl summed up the sales pitch of the American industrial designers when he wrote in 1932,

78 JACQUES PETERS Sportswear shop in the Bullock-Wilshire Department Store, ▶
Los Angeles, 1928

'successful styling implies progressive restyling'. The new image of the thirties was the aerodynamic streamlined form: with its implication of the futuristic Buck Rogers world, it provided – as did the Hollywood film and science fiction stories and comics – a much needed antidote to the greyness of the depression years.

By the time of the 1939 New York and San Francisco World Fairs, the Streamlined Moderne was, as Reyner Banham has indicated, on the brink of becoming the 'American Style'. Europe could boast of examples of Streamlined architecture, but the style was never as unified or as widespread as it was in America. The commercial parts of west Los Angeles came close to presenting a homogeneous Streamlined Moderne scene. The most prominent of these works were the NBC Building (John C. Austin & Co. and O. B. Hanson, 1939), the CBS Building (Lescaze and Heitschmidt, 1937–8), the May Co. 79 Department Store on Wilshire Boulevard (Albert Martin and S. A. Marx, 1940) and Coulter's Department Store, also on Wilshire (Stiles O. Clements, 1937).

Schindler was too evangelistic in his commitment to the true modern to embrace the Streamlined Moderne. As already mentioned, the industrial designers worked hard (and success-fully) to erase their image as artists, and to substitute that of the down-to-earth 'practical' – low art – designer-engineer. Schindler could not do this, but he was prepared to modify his buildings and take a few elements of the new fashion, and he tried (unsuccessfully) to refurbish his own image so that to the public he would appear as a more practical figure.

He worked with the industrial designers Kem Weber and J. R. Davidson in providing several exhibitions, epic for Southern California, of modern and Moderne architecture: the most famous of these was the 1932 show at the University of California's Los Angeles campus, which included Frank Lloyd Wright, Neutra, Weber, Davidson and Schindler. Schindler cooperated in presenting with Neutra an evening course at UCLA on modern architecture; and when in 1934 UCLA was

79   ALBERT MARTIN (WITH S. A. MARX) May Co. Department Store, Los Angeles,
1939–40

considering the formation of a Department of Architecture,
he was proposed for the chairmanship.

But in spite of all his efforts, he was never quite able to market
his refurbished image; he was still the artist-architect. He deeply
resented Neutra's rapid rise to international prominence, just
because it was what he wished for himself, and yet, somehow,
could not bring about.

These reactions to the world around him contained in a sense
the same contradictions and ambiguities which one finds in
his designs.

In 1931 he was bitterly disappointed to find that Neutra was to be included in the now famous exhibition of modern architecture being planned by Philip Johnson and Henry-Russell Hitchcock for the Museum of Modern Art in New York. (Earlier Schindler, Neutra and Weber had unsuccessfully tried to set up a separate California section at the annual exhibition of the Architectural League in New York.) Before the 1932 exhibition Schindler engaged in a pointed exchange with Philip Johnson. Schindler wrote, 'It seems to me that instead of showing late attempts of creative architecture it [the exhibition] tends toward concentrating on the so-called "International Style". If this is the case my work has no place in it. I am not a stylist, not a functionalist, nor any other sloganist. Each of my buildings deals with a different *architectural* problem, the existence of which has been forgotten in this period of Rational Mechanization. The question of whether a house is really a house is more important to me, than the fact that it is made of steel, glass, putty or hot air.' Johnson's tart answer was, 'From my knowledge of your work, my real opinion is that your work would not belong in this exhibition.' Thus ended Schindler's first encounter with the Museum of Modern Art. The next was in 1935 when he was included in the Museum's exhibition 'Modern Architecture in California', which toured the United States between 1936 and 1939.

Since Schindler's clients in the thirties directly or indirectly benefited from the booming motion picture industry, the depression did not have as drastic an effect on him as it did on many other architects. His practice in the twenties was in any case financially marginal, so that the thin years of the early thirties were not much different, except that they produced no single wealthy client such as the Lovells or Miss Barnsdall – clients who came close to retaining the continual services of an architect, as they might retain a lawyer or a physician. In the worst years of the depression (1929–33), Schindler was reasonably busy with commissions not only for remodellings and for several stores and restaurants, but also for an apartment house and for three of his most important houses – the Elliot house (1930), the Von Koerber house (1931) and the Oliver house (1933).

82–85, 94–96, 86–93

At this time his major concern with structure was to exploit fully the existing technology of the building industry, which meant the stucco-sheathed wood frame. He prided himself on having discovered the modular system as early as 1915; though it had been in use in the United States since the 1890s. In the thirties he sought to refine this system even more. In his paper 'Reference Frames in Space', written in 1932 (though not published until 1946), he formulated his use of the module. 'I have found', he wrote, 'that the four foot unit will satisfactorily fulfil all specifications.' He pointed out that, by the use of the four foot unit, detailed measurements could be dispensed with on the drawings, as those constructing the building need work only with multiples or divisions of the module. He argued that the vertical space in his designs was best realized through the use of the module: 'Room walls used to create space forms do not rise straight and boxlike from floor to ceiling, but may project or recess in between.' But while Schindler argued for a modular system, he did not wish to be rigidly tied to it. 'It is not necessary that the designer be completely enchained by the grid. I have found that occasionally a space-form may be improved by deviating slightly from the unit. Such sparing deviation does not invalidate the system as a whole but merely reveals the limits inherent in all mechanical schemes.' One has here technical 'truth' compromised by artistic considerations.

Schindler's modular system, as he developed it, was almost solely concerned with wood frame construction. He did use it, however, for two concrete schemes in 1933, the 'Schindler Shelters' and the first project for the Locke house. In 1929 and 1930 Schindler had worked with a friend, William Lingenbrink, in the speculative development of Park Moderne in the San Fernando Valley. While Schindler did not design the layout of this retreat in the hills he was certainly consulted. Two of his small wood frame houses were built at the Park Moderne,

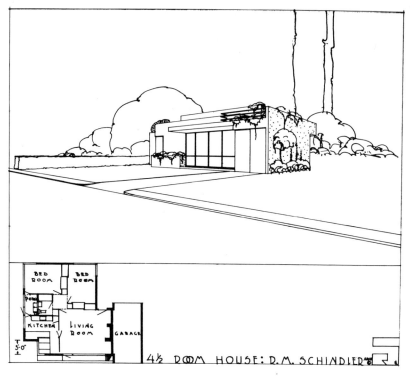

80   Schindler Shelter, project for a 4½ room concrete house, 1933

along with three Zigzag Moderne houses designed by others.
The 1929 crash virtually ended the project – it never really
recovered – but even so Schindler went on to plan a number of
small low-cost houses for it, some wood-framed and some of
concrete. He published these plus a few other designs as the
80   'Schindler Shelters' in the early thirties. He tried to have these
designs considered for one of the Federal Government's low-
cost housing programmes, but he met with the coldest of
bureaucratic receptions. In part this may have been a reaction
to their modern styling, but it was equally due to their cost,
$1,800 each, which could easily be undercut by a contractor-
built dwelling.

118

Schindler's last domestic design in concrete was his initial
scheme for the Eric Locke house at Los Angeles, of 1933; its 81
outward image is as close as he was ever to come to the industrial
Streamlined Moderne of the thirties. Instead of his usual
sharply defined 90° angle between vertical and horizontal surfaces, he joined these surfaces together with a gentle curve.
Floor, walls and ceiling thus suggest not separate forms, but a
single object poured in a single form. The integral concrete
seat of the living room runs through the glass wall toward the
garden, forming an outdoor seat, and at the other end of the
living room it penetrates through the inner glass wall which
separates the living and sleeping spaces to create a platform for
the bed. The separation of the house from the site is emphasized
by cantilevering the concrete floor slab (and sometimes the
wall as well) out over the ground.

81   First scheme for the Eric Locke house, Los Angeles, 1933

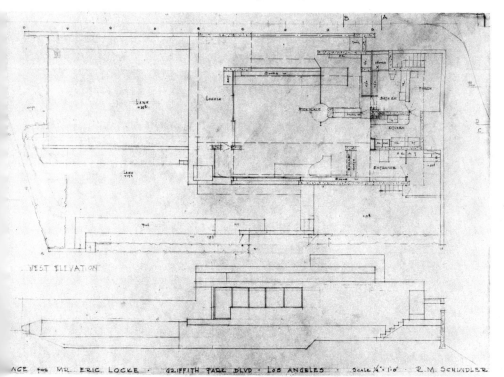

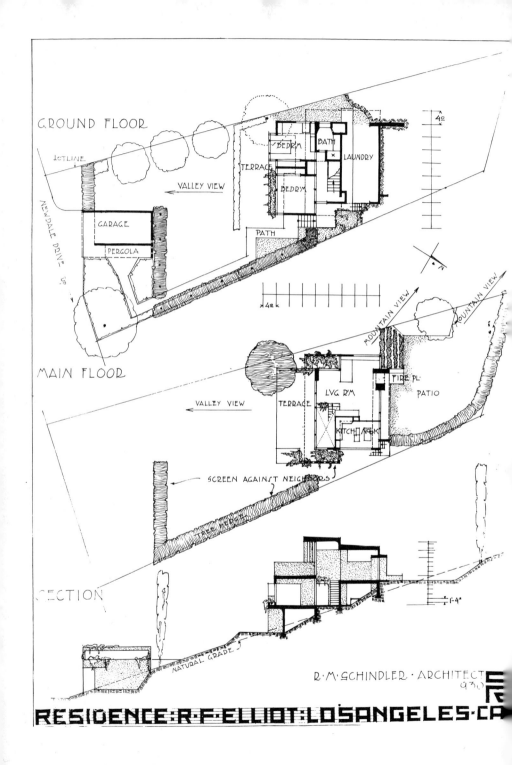

GROUND FLOOR

LOTLINE

NEWDALE DRIVE — UP.

GARAGE

PERGOLA

BEDR'M   PATH
TERRACE   LAUNDRY
BEDR'M

VALLEY VIEW

PATH

42

×42×

MAIN FLOOR

VALLEY VIEW   TERRACE   LVG R'M

MOUNTAIN VIEW   MOUNTAIN VIEW

FIRE PL·   PATIO

KITCH A5K·

SCREEN AGAINST NEIGHBORS

TREE HEDGE·

SECTION

NATURAL GRADE

1'-4"

R·M·SCHINDLER · ARCHITECT
930

RESIDENCE:R·F·ELLIOT:LOSANGELES·CA

CHAPTER NINE

Living space

With the R. F. Elliot house at Los Angeles (1930), Schindler *82–85*
began the full-blown application of his de Stijl aesthetic to the
hillside house. He placed the garage on street level at the base
of the hill. Suspended only a few feet above the garage is a
stucco-covered trellis, which, when covered with vines, would
appear a solid screen of green from the house above, near the
top of the site. The ground floor of the house contains the
entrance and sleeping area; on the second level above and
stepped back over the ground floor is the main living area. Glass
doors lead from the living-dining area to the front terrace over *84*
the lower bedrooms, which have a view of the valley below;
at the rear the interior space is continued outward through
fixed glass and glass doors to the outdoor living room, or patio.
High windows to the west give a glimpse of the distant mountains. The trellis motif of the garage is repeated to each side of
the living room, in this case to establish a partial visual barrier *84*
from the neighbouring houses.

The Elliot house is one of Schindler's most successful com-
binations of form and function. It is well sited, and the plan
admirably provides a flexible series of highly usable enclosed
and open spaces. Both visual and functionally the interior is
beautifully opened up to the exterior, while as a form, or series
of forms, it is complex both within and without. Like the
Wolfe house it floats above the hillside and is not perceptibly
connected to it, yet the window bases and trellises, with their
plants and vines, partially ensnare the surfaces and volumes and
bring them back to the ground. Within, the ground level is
attached to the upper main floor by the vertical, spatial exten- *83, 85*
sions of the entrance hall. While separate, the kitchen still
remains attached to the living-dining area, for they share a

◀ 82   House for R. F. Elliot, Los Angeles, 1930: plans and section

83   House for R.F. Elliot, Los Angeles, 1930: living room (note the staircase at right, seen in Ill. 85)

84 House for R. F. Elliot, Los Angeles, 1930; bedrooms with front terrace over

continuous ceiling which penetrates the partial glass barrier
placed between them. The living-dining room is covered by
three separate ceiling-roofs which step down to form the more
intimate space leading on to the rear patio. Schindler used the
most common and readily available materials for both structure
and finishes: stucco (inside and out), plain fir plywood (waxed,
not varnished or painted) and linoleum for floors and table
tops.

86, 87   Directly after the Elliot house in 1931, Schindler prepared
his scheme for the first W. E. Oliver house at Los Angeles. Here
the site was reversed: the street and garage are at the top, and the
house is down below on the slope. The main living space is
again above, while the bedrooms are below at ground level.
The two-storey connective space for the Elliot house is enlarged
into an L shape, overlooking a sunken garden; and the children's
bedrooms below are separated from the double-height hall and

the sunken garden by fixed glass and glass doors. At the upper level of the site a bridge connects the garden and the roof-terrace on top of the garage with a rear deck which overlooks the valley.

Before the working drawings were started for this first scheme the Olivers purchased another site closer to the city, with superb views across Silver Lake to the rear and, in front, across west Los Angeles to the ocean. As it was finally built in 1933, *88–90,* the house is on a single floor, with the garage below at street *92, 93* level. The L-shaped building is placed obliquely on its plot so that it can make the most of its three views and also have the maximum use of the flat ground to the rear made into a patio. *92* A small entrance hall is situated five feet below the main floor level. The living and dining space and the kitchen occupy the front, and the children's room the rear, with the parents' room and a porch between. A roof terrace was placed on top of the children's room where it was planned to provide for another bedroom, never in fact built. Entrance to the children's wing is through the porch; thus an effective separation is provided between the three zones of the house.

The Oliver house, however, seems to be made up of several intentional contradictions, the most surprising of which is that it looks like a flat-roofed box from the street below. In actual fact it is covered by shed and gable roofs, which are fully *90* revealed on the garden side; these varied roofs enabled Schindler to change the ceiling heights dramatically throughout the *93* house. The introduction of shed and gable roofs into a sharp right-angled de Stijl composition is the deliberate sort of ambiguity which he returned to again and again during the thirties and after. (Loos, of course, created a similar sense of ambiguity between his sharp clear right-angle compositions and his curved roofs.) In some instances the slant roof had to be *91* introduced (and if possible denied at the same time) because of local style restraints, aimed at furthering the cause of the Spanish Colonial Revival; but in most cases it was chosen deliberately by Schindler.

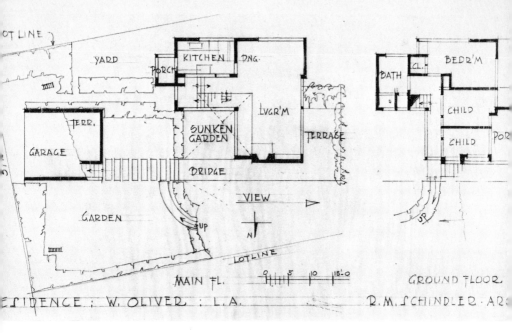

Labels in the upper plan drawing:

OT LINE
YARD KITCHEN DNG.
PORCH
TERR.
SUNKEN GARDEN
GARAGE
LVGR'M
TERRACE
BRIDGE
GARDEN
VIEW
UP
N
LOTLINE
MAIN FL.   0   5   10   15'0"
ESIDENCE: W. OLIVER: L.A.

BATH CL. BEDR'M
CHILD
CHILD POR
UP
GROUND FLOOR
R.M. SCHINDLER · AR

86, 87   First scheme for the W. E. Oliver house, Los Angeles, 1931: above, plans; below, perspective view from the garden (bottom left in plan)

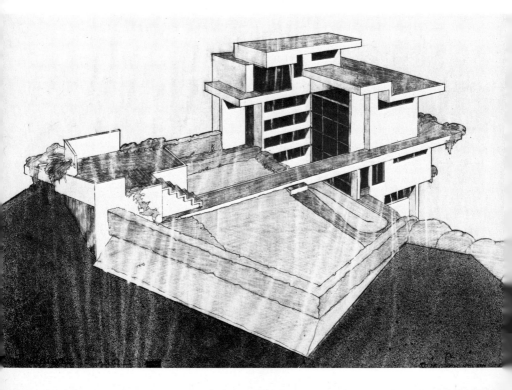

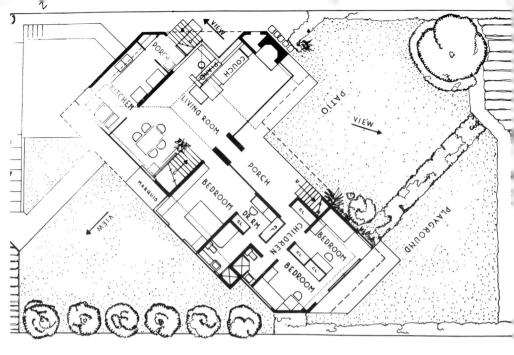

88, 89   House for W. E. Oliver, Los Angeles, 1933: above, plan; below, view from the street (upper left in plan)

90　House for W. E. Oliver, Los Angeles, 1933: view from the garden

91　ADOLF LOOS Steiner house, Vienna, 1910

92, 93   House for W. E. Oliver, Los Angeles, 1933: above, view from living room toward patio and porch; below, living room

94, 95 House for Hans N. Von Koerber, Hollywood Riviera, Torrance, 1931: above, clerestory window; below, entrance

96   House for
Hans N. Von
Koerber, Hollywood
Riviera,
Torrance, 1931:
living room
fireplace

The house built in 1931 for Hans N. Von Koerber, in the
Spanish Colonial Revival community of the Hollywood
Riviera, was Schindler's most openly satirical comment on the
Hispanic Revival. The rectangular geometry of the vertical surfaces of the house is uncompromisingly de Stijl; but the whole
building is covered by what seems at first glance to be a confused array of tile-covered shed roofs, several of which pour   94, 95
their tile coverings over and down the adjacent walls. Within,
the fireplace is covered with vertical rows of roofing tile; while   96
the hearth boasts rows of curved roofing tiles with their con-
cave surfaces facing upwards. The interior, with its involved
changes of floor and ceiling levels emphasized by the varied
placement of windows and electric light sources, is at odds not
only with the doctrine of austerity of the International Style but
also with the chaste interior space of the Spanish Colonial
Revival.

131

Equally undoctrinaire was the **A**-frame cabin for Gisela
97 Bennati at Lake Arrowhead (1934–7), mentioned above. The
local restrictive style here was 'French Norman', which, what-
ever else it might imply, meant that the houses must be roofey.
Schindler responded characteristically, as he had earlier in the
Packard house, by making the cabin *all* roof – a thrust at
regulations and conventionality, but also personally consistent
in view of his continual use of angled walls and roofs.

Far more acceptable to the Internationalists, because of their
rectilinear purism, were two designs of 1934 for Los Angeles:
a projected house at Leimert Park, and a house for John J. Buck.

97 Mountain cabin for Gisela Bennati, Lake Arrowhead, 1934–7

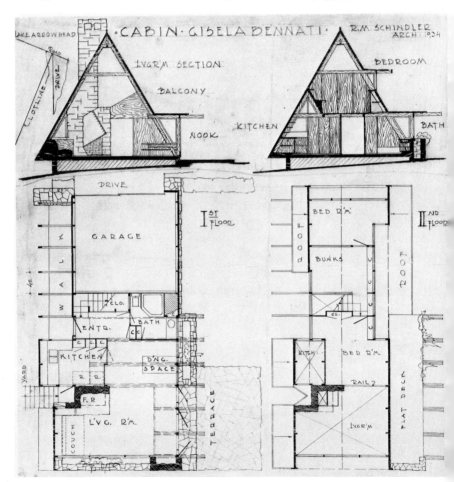

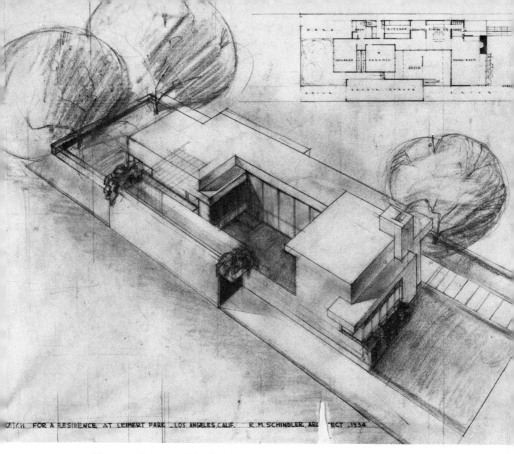

98 Projected house at Leimert Park, Los Angeles, 1934

Both were designed for flat city sites; and perhaps the blandness of the sites and of the surrounding buildings suggested that here he could compose exclusively in a vocabulary of right angles. In the Buck house the rectangular volumes and the *99, 100* horizontal bands of windows are terminated by the verticality of the two chimneys. The height of the interior space is varied so that light can enter at several levels, and the ceiling of the entrance hall is pulled down twenty-four inches below the flat roof plane, so that one can see right through the house.

The small projected house at Leimert Park is not so theatrical *98* an object in space, but the treatment of volumes is close to that of the Buck house.

While the visual impact of the two houses, particularly the Buck, is impressively photogenic, their real contribution lies

99, 100 in their admirable, functional plans. The **L**-shaped Buck house, which is really two houses, as there is a small apartment for rental over the garage, opens and extends most of its rooms out on to a secluded patio; the Leimert Park house organizes itself around a small inner courtyard, with the breakfast, dining and living spaces – and even the kitchen through a glass wall – treated as a contiguous open space which freely spreads into the patio. This open and free interior space, and its visual-utilitarian extension into outdoor living rooms, anticipated certain aspects of the work in the later thirties of the Bay Area School of Wurster, Funk and Dailey, and, in Los Angeles, of Ain, Soriano and Harris.

Schindler's closest approximation to Neutra's classic stucco-glass volumes was his design for the W.J. Delahoyde house on

101 a hillside at Los Angeles (1935). Here the two-storey form is static, but the layered volumes thrust themselves in and out. The design of the stairs to the street-level garage, with a cut-out wall above, is more de Stijl than the house itself.

99 House for John J. Buck, Los Angeles, 1934

RESIDENCE OF:
MR. & MRS. J. J. BUCK
LOS ANGELES, CALIF.
R.M. SCHINDLER, ARCHITECT
1 9 3 4.

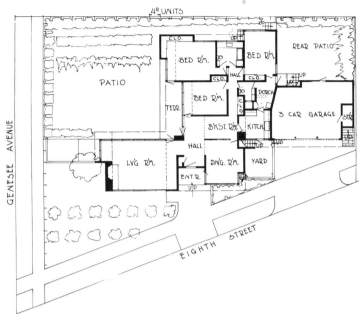

100   House for John J. Buck, Los Angeles, 1934: plans

101   Projected house for W.J. Delahoyde, Los Angeles, 1935

RESIDENCE : MR·AND·MRS· DELAHOYDE : R·M· SCHINDLER·ARCH·193

The street elevation of the second scheme for the Milton Shep house at Los Angeles (1935) is close to the International Style; but a much more characteristic arrangement of projecting, receding and interlocking volumes occurs on the elevation to the hillside. In the first scheme for the Geggie house at Pasadena (1935–6), the two shed roofs are so strong that they radically modify the de Stijl walls below. In this house Schindler not only made no attempt in a traditional classical fashion to resolve the conflict between the volumes dominated by the shed roofs and the volumes contained by the rectangular roof surfaces, but actually exploited the clash of these elements as the theme of the design.

102   Second scheme for the Milton Shep house, Los Angeles, 1935: garden front

103 First scheme for the Morris Geggie house, Pasadena, 1935–6

In the years immediately following the Geggie design, he extended this open battle of forms in the projects for the Warshaw house at Los Angeles and the William Jacobs house at Beverly Glen, both of 1936. In these two projects he contained his in-and-out de Stijl volumes within a curved roof highly suggestive of the streamlined packaging of the Moderne objects of the thirties. In the Warshaw design the slightly slanted roof, articulated by wooden bands, curves down to become the rear wall; in the Jacobs house the curve extends to include the clerestory windows, and the bands continue on to the soffit and the ceiling inside. The tying of roof and wall together by the use of roofing paper and wood bands had, of course, been used in the 1924 Packard house, and Schindler had recently employed this device in the John DeKeyser double house at Hollywood (1935). The Warshaw and Jacobs projects were, however, the only occasions on which curved continuous surfaces were used to hold a de Stijl composition in place.

104, 105

34

137

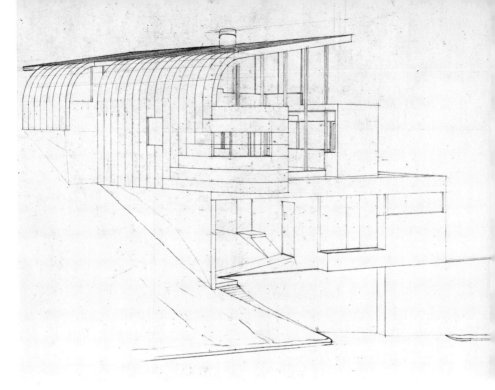

104   Projected house for Warshaw, Los Angeles, 1936

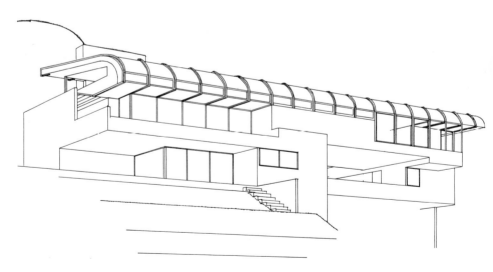

105   Second scheme for the William Jacobs house, Beverly Glen, 1936

Modern versus Moderne

The mid-thirties marked another turning point, not only for Schindler but for American architecture in general. In 1936 Wright re-emerged with great and unexpected vigour in his Administration Building for the Johnson Wax Co. at Racine, Wisconsin, and Falling Water for the Kaufmann family at Bear Run, Pennsylvania. In California, Neutra brought forth in 1935 his open-air school at Bell and his prefabricated metal *106* house in Altadena; and a year earlier the young Harwell H. Harris (with Carl Anderson) built the courtyard-oriented Lowe *108* house, also in Altadena. Two other young designers were then beginning to make their mark on the Los Angeles scene: Gregory Ain, with his Edwards house (1936) and Raphael *109* Soriano, with his Lipetz house (1935). In Northern California, *107* William Wurster, Gardner Dailey, John Funk, Mario Corbett, Francis McCarthy and John Dinwiddie were beginning to converge into a movement which matured just before the Second World War.

With the exception of this 'woodsy' Bay Region group (and Harris' buildings in the Southland) the visual image of American architecture which set the fashion in the thirties was the stream-lined transportation machine. Wright and Schindler could think of nothing more repugnant than that their work might share elements of what they both considered the slick stream-lining of Norman Bel Geddes or Raymond Loewy, but share them it did. Wright's Johnson Wax Co. has a strong suggestion of the industrially designed object, and while Schindler did not compromise his commitment to the right-angle and flat plane, the curved surface cropped up increasingly in his furniture and in occasional examples of decorative art which found their way into his houses. Neutra and Wright continued to employ the

106 RICHARD J. NEUTRA Corona Avenue School, Bell, 1935

107 RAPHAEL S. SORIANO Lipetz house, Los Angeles, 1935

108   HARWELL H. HARRIS (WITH CARL ANDERSON) House for Pauline Lowe, Altadena, 1934

109   GREGORY AIN Edwards house, Los Angeles, 1936

curve throughout the thirties, but they integrated the streamline into the totality of their designs. Schindler as usual posed it as an antithesis in open and glaring contrast to rectangular forms.

Schindler's effort to improve his public relations image would seem in 1935 and 1936 to have started to pay off. Economically Hollywood was on the upswing, and there was emerging an even larger clientèle which wanted the latest in the modern mode. Most of these clients (who were more often women than men) ended up merely with the Moderne, but the radical-left in fashion craved for something more genuinely modern than glass brick, curved façades and flat roofs. Here Schindler, and to an even greater extent Neutra, entered the picture: joined by Ain and Soriano, they created a design product which appeared, and in fact was, much more uncompromising in its commitment to twentieth-century high art than the Moderne. Of the two, Neutra's outward packaging was the more unflinching in its reflection of the impersonal machine. Schindler's machine aesthetic of the mid and late thirties was more confused, since it was based on images derived from both high art and low art; therefore it could never have the impressive instantaneous impact of Neutra. A few perceptive clients sensed that of all the avant-garde architects practising in Los Angeles, Schindler was the most revolutionary – as was clearly apparent in a group of six houses which he designed during 1934–6. There are two hillside houses in Los Angeles *110–112,* itself, the Elizabeth Van Patten house (1934–5) and the Ralph *113–115* G. Walker house (1935–6). On the street side of the Van Patten house one sees only three attached garages, each stepped back from the other and each covered by a shed roof, the total effect *110* being akin to a saw-tooth factory roof. The three-storey house hidden behind the garages is covered by two wide shed roofs oppositely pitched, and a single flat roof. The pitch of the main shed roof is repeated in the ramp leading to the lower deck and *112* in the angled base of the second floor deck. The street front of the Walker house, with its simple rectangular shape and row

110, 111   House for Elizabeth Van Patten, Silver Lake, Los Angeles, 1934–5: above, street-level garages; below, living room

112   House for Elizabeth Van Patten, Silver Lake, Los Angeles, 1934–5: exterior showing angled decks

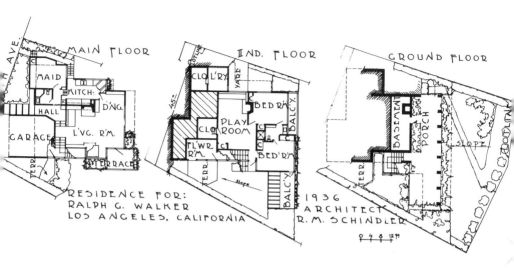

MAIN FLOOR   IIND. FLOOR   GROUND FLOOR

RESIDENCE FOR:
RALPH G. WALKER
LOS ANGELES, CALIFORNIA

1936
ARCHITECT
R. M. SCHINDLER

113, 114   House for Ralph G. Walker, Los Angeles, 1935–6: above, plans; below, living-dining room

115   House for Ralph G. Walker, Los Angeles, 1935–6: garden front

of strip windows under the eaves, is International Style in feeling, while the rear of the house with its eight supporting concrete piers, horizontal trellis, deck and roof is completely Schindler-esque de Stijl. *115*

More full-blown in their de Stijl atmosphere were the house projects for Milton Shep at Los Angeles (1935) and for Morris Geggie at Pasadena (1935–6), and the beach house project for Rupert R. Ryan at an unknown location (1937). Key-shaped volumes project and recede in each of these houses, tying walls, roofs and windows together and at the same time providing a forceful connection between interior and exterior space. In three of these houses he used flat roofs – though in the Geggie project he placed a second shed roof over the house as a sun-shade. To gain full advantage of views and sunlight in the Shep design, he angled the house in relation to the street and then, because of the legally required set-backs, calmly sliced off portions of his right-angled volumes (without in any way compromising the usefulness of interior space); this shift away from pure right-angled geometry introduced another dis-quieting note into his designs. *102, 103* *116*

116   Projected beach house for Rupert R. Ryan, 1937

As a piece of architectural sculpture, embracing the full range of his de Stijl aesthetic, Schindler's great work of the mid-thirties was the house for Victoria McAlmon at Los Angeles (1935–6). Here out of a single L-shaped volume he pro-
117 jected secondary volumes, interlocked key motifs and slab roofs, all carefully connected by the contrasting volumes. Every projecting wall, roof slab and window opening was treated as an element in the total design. In some sections of the house, such as the entrance and the rear dining porch, exterior spaces penetrate within; in other instances closed and open interior
118 space projects outward.

Yet, for all its intense concern with aesthetics, there is no sense of compromise in the plan of the McAlmon house. The long, narrow site sloped gently from the street and then folded sharply up and over the ridge. Schindler moved an existing bungalow to the front of the property, placed a garage under it and clothed it in a de Stijl shell. The new main house was then situated on top of the ridge, with all the major rooms opening out to the view.

117   House for Victoria McAlmon, Los Angeles, 1935: street front

118   House for Victoria McAlmon, Los Angeles, 1935: living room

Equally de Stijl is the C. C. Fitzpatrick house at Los Angeles *119–121* (1936), but here the layers of horizontal roof slabs are stronger than the volumes below. This house was meant to be theatrical, for it was built as a come-on for new speculative land development at the top of the Hollywood hills.

The four years from 1936 to 1939 mark the high point of Southern California's first adventures in the International Style. Neutra produced his metal-clad Von Sternberg house at Northridge in 1936 and his Miller house at Palm Springs in *122, 123* 1938. The younger Soriano designed the Ross house at Los Angeles in 1938 and the Kimpson-Nixon house at Long Beach *124* in 1939. Even H. H. Harris turned Internationalist in his house at Pacific Palisades (1937) for John Entenza, the editor and publisher of *Arts and Architecture*.

Equally modern, if not Moderne, were the stores, offices and private houses of J. R. Davidson (for example his Stothart house *125* of 1937 in Santa Monica), and of Kem Weber (see the Wedemeyer house at Altadena, also of 1937). These in turn were *126* followed after the war by Entenza's impressive case-study house programme.

149

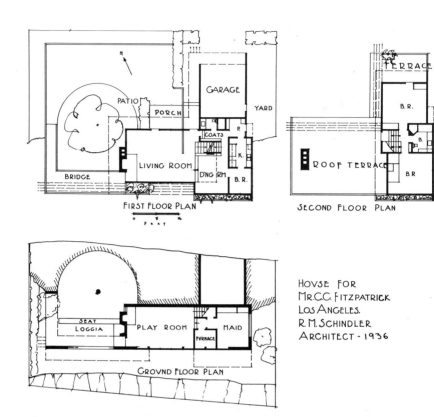

FIRST FLOOR PLAN

SECOND FLOOR PLAN

GROVND FLOOR PLAN

HOVSE FOR
Mr. C.C. FITZPATRICK
LOS ANGELES.
R.M. SCHINDLER
ARCHITECT - 1936

119, 120 House for C. C. Fitzpatrick, Los Angeles, 1936: above, plans; below, living room

121 House for C. C. Fitzpatrick, Los Angeles, 1936: hillside front

122 RICHARD J. NEUTRA Von Sternberg house, Northridge, 1936

123   RICHARD J. NEUTRA Miller house, Palm Springs, 1938

124   RAPHAEL S. SORIANO Kimpson-Nixon house, Long Beach, 1939

125 J.R. Davidson Stothart-Phillips house, Santa Monica, 1937: terrace

126 Kem Weber Wedemeyer house, Altadena, 1937

127 House for Henwar Rodakiewicz, Los Angeles, 1937: garden front

As with the Moderne, Schindler could never bring himself to use the International Style entirely, yet he did manage to design two houses which utilized quite a number of details and materials which had come to characterize its American version. These two houses were the large Henwar Rodakiewicz house at Los Angeles (1937) and the studio-house for Hilaire Hiler at Hollywood (1941). In the Rodakiewicz house he was provided with a large-scale opportunity to realize his three-dimensional view of interior space and how that space might be extended into the surrounding landscape. The stairway of the ground-level entrance leads directly into the double-volume living room, which has a high glass-enclosed loggia to one side and a view of the semi-circular patio through the floor-to-ceiling glass windows. A staircase in the internal loggia leads up to the main bedrooms and on to a balcony, from which a curved bridge penetrates through the glass and forms one side of the sunken patio. The precision of the detailing, with polished metal for window mullions and railings, has a nautical, machine-like quality.

127–129

131, 132

129

127

128 House for Henwar Rodakiewicz, Los Angeles, 1937: plans ▶

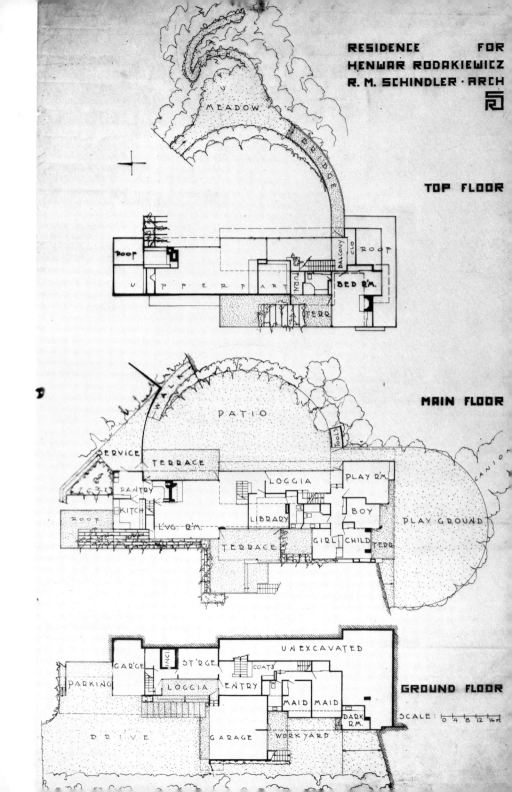

RESIDENCE FOR
HENWAR RODAKIEWICZ
R. M. SCHINDLER · ARCH

TOP FLOOR

MEADOW

BRIDGE

ROOF

ROOF

UPPER PART

BALCONY

CLO

BED R'M

TURN

TERR

MAIN FLOOR

WALK

PATIO

CANION

SERVICE

TERRACE

LOGGIA

PLAY R'M

COOL

PANTRY

KITCH

ROOF

L'VG R'M

LIBRARY

BOY

PLAY GROUND

TERRACE

GIRL

CHILD

TERR

GROUND FLOOR

GAR'GE

INCL

ST'R'GE

COATS

UNEXCAVATED

PARKING

LOGGIA

ENTRY

MAID

MAID

SCALE: 0 4 8 12 16 ft

DRIVE

GARAGE

WORKYARD

DARK
R'M

129 House for Henwar Rodakiewicz, Los Angeles, 1937: living room

130 House for Rose L. Harris, Los Angeles, 1942

The garden of the Rodakiewicz house exemplifies Schindler's view that the surrounding landscape should be left alone, thereby contrasting with the building. The semi-circular patio to the east of the house and the semi-circular children's playground below, to the south, are handled as direct, controlled extensions of interior spaces. Beyond these two precisely bound areas is a twentieth-century version of the romantic English garden: a meadow, a winding grass path and plantings of trees and shrubs to suggest a dense jungle. Out of this irregularity and wildness rises the man-made geometry of the house. Schindler's most complete version of the English picturesque landscape in relation to the controlled works of man is in his later Rose L. Harris house at Los Angeles (1942), where he *130* precariously perched the house and its partially enclosed patio directly on top of an irregular rock outcropping.

The second of his International Style designs was the Hiler studio-house. This is a real town house, located only a short block off Sunset Boulevard. The garages are set below it, at right angles to the street; above, placed centrally in the house, is a double-volume studio-living room, lit by extensive skylights with baffles suspended below to diffuse the sunlight. Though less metal shows in the Hiler studio-house, its exterior-interior image is still that of machine packaging. Like the industrial products of the period, it conveys a feeling of being not designed but styled, a form superimposed on workings.

131   Studio-house for Hilaire Hiler, Hollywood, 1941

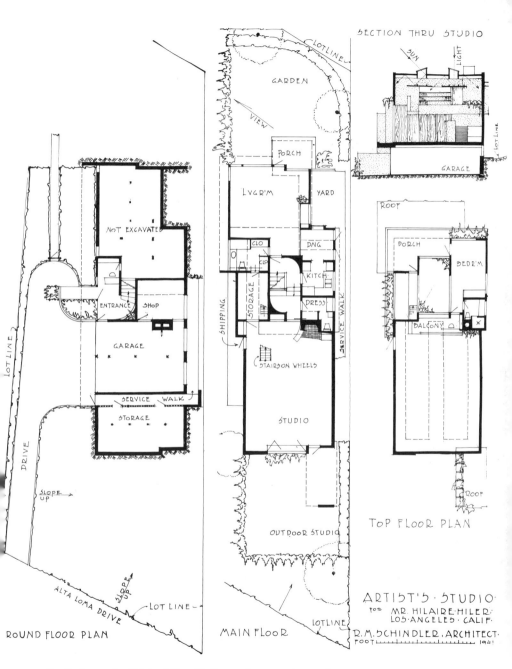

SECTION THRU STUDIO

SUN   LIGHT

GARAGE

GARDEN

VIEW

LOT LINE

PORCH

LVGR'M   YARD

NOT EXCAVATED

CLO

CLS   DNG

STORAGE   KITCH

DRESS

SHIPPING

SERVICE WALK

ENTRANCE   SHOP

GARAGE

STAIRS ON WHEELS

SERVICE WALK

STORAGE

STUDIO

LOT LINE

DRIVE

SLOPE UP

OUTDOOR STUDIO

LOT LINE

ALTA LOMA DRIVE   SLOPE UP   LOT LINE

ROUND FLOOR PLAN

MAIN FLOOR

ROOF

PORCH

BEDR'M

BALCONY

ROOF

TOP FLOOR PLAN

ARTIST'S · STUDIO·
FOR MR· HILAIRE· HILER·
LOS· ANGELES · CALIF·
R· M· SCHINDLER · ARCHITECT·
FOOT   1941

132   Studio-house for Hilaire Hiler, Hollywood, 1941: plans and section

Before the war and in its early years, Schindler applied his late de Stijl aesthetic to the Selmer Westby house at Los Angeles (1938), the Henry J. Wolff house at Studio City (1938), the G.J. Droste house at Hollywood (1940), the Samuel Goodwin house at Studio City (1940) and the remodelling of the John Pennington house at Thousand Oaks (1942). Another aspect of his de Stijl packaging was his use, in 1938, of modular plywood for several houses in Los Angeles: in the projected E. Djey-M. Aldrich house, the vertically placed plywood panels establish the structural and aesthetic module of the building; in the Mildred Southall studio-house, the vertical joints of the plywood sheets are almost concealed, so that the internal and external surfaces read as a continuous plane.

CHAPTER ELEVEN

Business commissions

By late 1941 whole streets in Los Angeles, especially in the western commercial area, were dotted with Streamlined Moderne buildings. The most impressive and largest of these were designed by the offices of Stiles O. Clements and of Albert Martin. The Streamlined Moderne was used for every conceivable type of building, ranging from Ralph's Supermarkets, designed by Stiles O. Clements and Associates, to motion picture theatres such as S. Charles Lee's Academy Theatre at Inglewood (1939). While all of the modern Los Angeles architects – Schindler, Neutra, Ain, Soriano and Harris – had their fingers occasionally in this commercial pot, the number and size of the commissions they received were small. As in the twenties the explanation for the dearth of commissions lay both in their lack of rapport with the business community and in the novelty of their styling.

Schindler's most substantial commercial commissions were for Sardi's Restaurant No. 1 and Lindy's Restaurant No. 1, both of 1932–4 and in Hollywood. The use of polished metal surfaces and structural members in both of these restaurants continued the machine-like quality of his earlier Braxton *68, 69* Gallery (1928) and the projected store front for J. J. Newberry at Los Angeles (1929). All of these buildings could be open advertisements for the modern, and Schindler made the most of this. He designed a wide variety of indirect lighting sources for Sardi's Restaurant – below seats, behind cases and built-in seats, in coving, where it was deflected by metal or even mirror lining. With the curve and T-square, he tried his hand at typefaces which in theory would be readable and at the same time would dramatically attract attention. The external lettering at *133* Sardi's (for which he also designed the menu cards) is certainly the most satisfactory of these typefaces.

◀ 133   Sardi's Restaurant No. 1, Hollywood, 1932–4: detail of street front

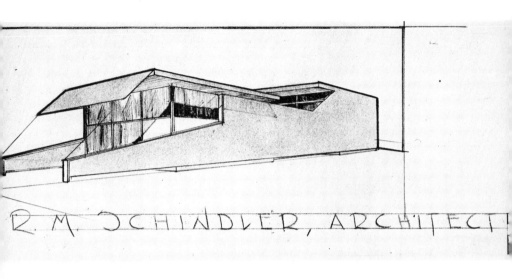

134, 135   Projected beach colony for A.E. Rose, Santa Monica, 1937: above, individual house; below, general view

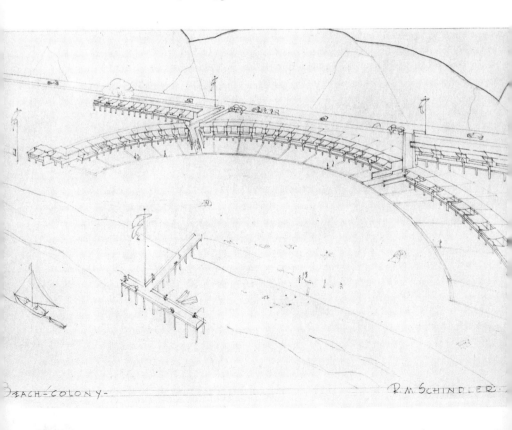

The precision of the machine was, appropriately, the mood of Schindler's three designs for service stations – a prototype model for the Standard Oil Company (1932), a similar model for the Union Oil Company (1933), and a station for Mrs Nerenbaum, probably at Los Angeles (1934). His design for the Union Oil station, with its many intersecting beams and *136* surfaces, is a piece of de Stijl sculpture, while the station for Mrs Nerenbaum is a classic, almost Mondrian billboard.

The blank in Schindler's productive upswing of the thirties is in the field of multiple housing; yet it was an area of design that really interested him, and he grasped at every opportunity, no matter how remote. Until the end of the thirties, the closest he came to getting a housing group built was with the beach colony for A. E. Rose, probably at Santa Monica (1937). The colony was to consist of a large number of wood-framed, canvas- and stucco-covered beach houses which would be *134* rented for summer use. The arrangement in an open semi-circle has a strong hint of the Beaux Arts, but in this case it was a *135* scheme which worked, for it allowed each house to open on to the common area and have a view of the ocean. A small-scale portable mock-up was made of one of the beach houses. In the end the project was abandoned, because of the high cost of beach frontage property.

136   Prototype service station for the Union Oil Company, Los Angeles, 1933

In the apartment house for Pearl Mackey at Los Angeles (1939), each apartment has its own private outdoor living area, either a patio or a roof garden. The hillside location of the

137, 138 A. L. Bubeshko apartments, also at Los Angeles (built in two stages, 1938 and 1941), gave him more freedom, and he stepped the three floors of apartments up the slope. The set-back of each level made it possible to continue the internal spaces outward on to roof terraces and patios. The S. T. Falk apartments at Los Angeles (1939) twist and turn to take full advantage of a difficult site. Again each living unit has its own garden and roof terrace.

In 1942, after America had entered the Second World War,

139–142 Schindler designed another apartment house for Mrs S. T. Falk, for a hillside location in Los Angeles west of Silver Lake (which by this time had become a haven for modern and Moderne architecture). In this scheme he angled each apartment so as

142 to take in the view and the sunlight from the south; the stepped

141 angling means that each has a patio-deck private from the rest. The secondary spaces of each apartment are assembled around a double-volume living room. Here once again is the traditional double-volume studio house, but with a special twist which makes it something else: for the interiors of each apartment are not a volumetric box, with layered space above and below a balcony, but a complex vertical and horizontal space which

139 forcefully ties all the parts together.

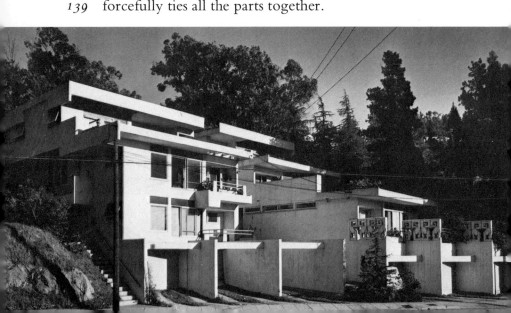

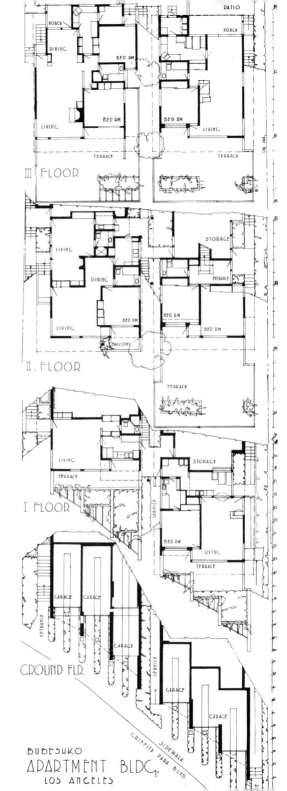

137, 138   Apartment
building for A.L. Bubeshko,
Los Angeles, 1938 and 1941:
opposite, street front;
right, plans

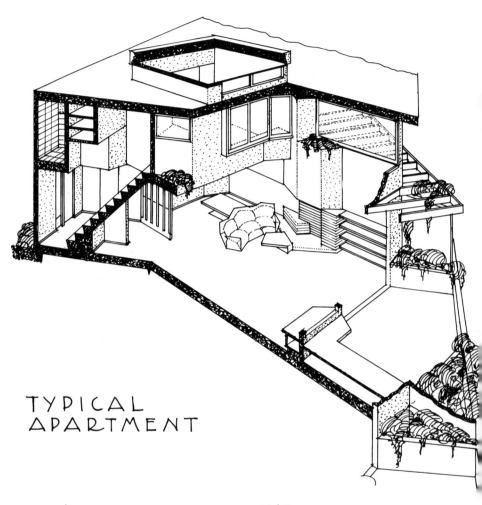

TYPICAL
APARTMENT

R.M. SCHINDLER · ARCHITECT · 1943·

139, 140 Project for apartment building for Mrs S.T. Falk, Los Angeles, 1942:
above, cross-section of typical apartment; opposite, plans of typical apartment

166

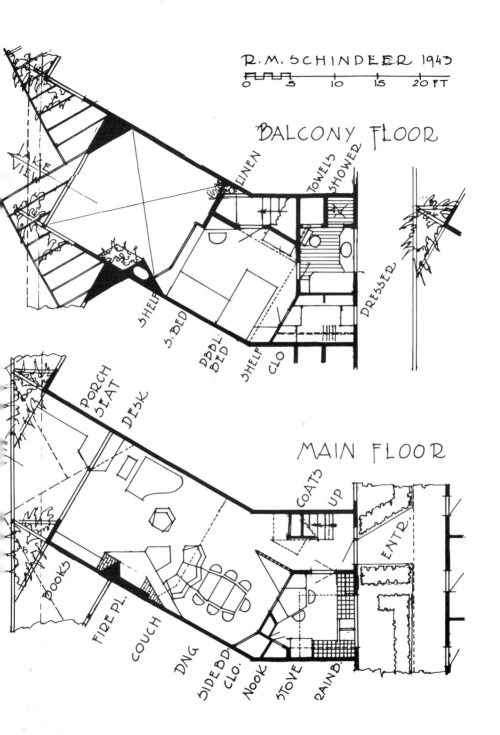

R. M. SCHINDEER 1943

0 ··· 5 ··· 10 ··· 15 ··· 20 FT

BALCONY FLOOR

LAKE VIEW

LINEN

TOWELS
SHOWER

DRESSER

SHELF
S. BED
DBBL. BED
SHELF CLO

PORCH SEAT
DESK

MAIN FLOOR

COATS
UP

ENTR.

BOOKS

FIRE PL.
COUCH
DNG
SIDE BD. CLO.
NOOK
STOVE
RAINB.

141, 142   Apartment house for Mrs S. T. Falk, Los Angeles, 1939: above, living room
of one apartment; below, view from lower street

CHAPTER TWELVE

The uses of wood

Schindler had argued strongly in the early and mid-thirties that external exposed wood was illogical in Southern California and that the stucco-covered box was visually and structurally consistent with the environment. His arguments were sound: there are nine months or so when there may not be a drop of rain, and the heavy winter rain and high humidity which follows make it difficult for any wood, including redwood, to stand up for any length of time. Economically, stucco remained the most practical and also the least expensive method of clothing the frame – even plywood could not compete.

By the late thirties he began to re-introduce wood for surfaces and exposed structure. This return to wood sheathing and occasional exposure of the wood structure was, although Schindler later denied it, a partial return to tradition and to his Constructivist work of the twenties. But there were several other advantages to wood; plywood was just starting to be mass-produced in quantities, at prices which made it practical for the construction of houses. For the modern architect plywood had another advantage: it could pose both as wood, and thus a traditional material, and as a new industrial product, one which in the thirties was being promoted in popular and technical journals. There was also fashion: the 'woodsy' buildings of the Bay Region architects (and in the south of H. H. Harris) had become by 1938–9 the modish thing in domestic architecture, and their popular success certainly tempted Schindler, and also Neutra, to go in the same direction. Neutra, with his self-limited forms, would use wood only for sheathing and for occasional projecting outriggers; but he promoted plywood as sheathing in his 1936 Plywood Model house, and he used redwood boards in his three small houses at Los Altos in 1935.

By 1940 Schindler had made plywood one of his principal materials. He experimented with its external use in his Haines house at Dana Point (1934–5) and in a number of other designs in the late thirties and forties. Internally he used it extensively for walls and for built-in cabinets and furniture. He preferred fir plywood (which he used in furniture for B. Inaya and many others) not only because it was the cheapest, but because it looked common and inexpensive. He designed more and more

143 of his furniture in plywood in such a way that it could easily be built by the carpenter on the job, rather than by a cabinet-maker. In this he was similar to Ain, but radically different from Neutra and Weber, and later Eames, all of whom sought to design furniture which would express and be a product of the machine.

143   Living room furniture designed for Milton Shep, Los Angeles, 1934–5

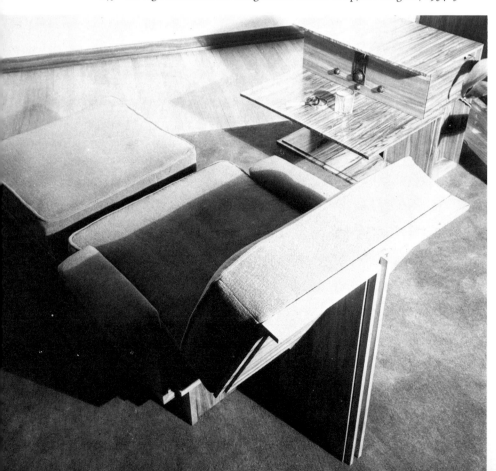

Schindler became increasingly interested in exposing wood structure for visual tension, but with the exception of the Olga Zaczek beach house at Playa del Rey (1936–8) he never liked to *149* use the more traditional redwood boards as vertical or horizontal weatherboarding. While Schindler was interested in the work of Wurster, Dailey and other Bay Region designers, it is more likely that he was encouraged to use exposed wood by the concurrent work in Los Angeles of Harris, Ain and Lloyd Wright; he could not avoid responding to the wood structured and sheathed Usonian houses which Frank Lloyd Wright was then producing.

For the proponents of modern architecture, the increased use of wood and increased prominence of gabled and shed roofs in Schindler's work must have seemed a regrettable anti-de Stijl reversion to the early twenties. But these discordant elements had always remained essential to his work: even during the height of his de Stijl period he had superimposed a variety of roof forms on the Oliver, Van Patten and Walker *90, 112* houses. His 1938 house for Guy C. Wilson, with its increased *115, 144* use of wood and its upturned shed roof, really belongs with these three earlier houses. But the second house for C. P. Lowes at Eagle Rock (1937), the project for the Arthur R. Timme house at Los Angeles (1938), the Albert Van Dekker house at

Canoga Park (1940) and the J. Rodriguez house at Glendale (1941) represent something quite different. In these houses the roof and often its exposed wood structure overshadow the

145 rectangular de Stijl composition below. In the Rodriguez house, angled U struts envelop the band of living room windows: projecting outward from the base of the windows, they are carried up at an angle, and then turn again to become the rafters.

146–148 The roof itself is hung below the rafters. In the Van Dekker house, such structural gymnastics are confined to the interior; externally the various shed and gable roofs (covered with copper and wood battens) are treated visually as angled planes. In all of these houses Schindler employed a shed or gable roof as a solution to the problem of vertical space internally, not for its picturesque qualities externally.

145   House for J. Rodriguez, Glendale, 1941

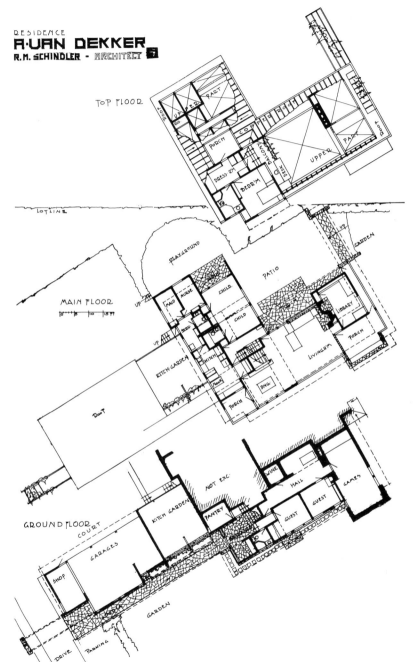

RESIDENCE
A·VAN DEKKER
R.M. SCHINDLER · ARCHITECT 5

TOP FLOOR

146 House for
Albert Van
Dekker, Canoga
Park, 1940: plans

MAIN FLOOR

GROUND FLOOR

147, 148 House for Albert Van Dekker, Canoga Park, 1940: above, exterior; below, living room

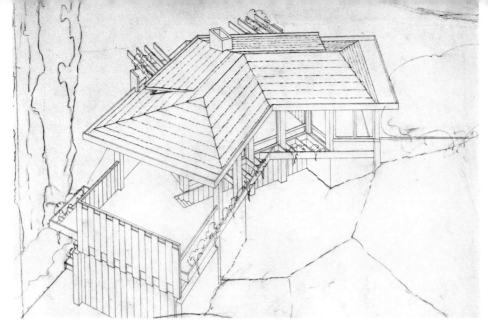

149 Beach house for Olga Zaczek, Playa del Rey, 1936–8

His closest approximation to the 'woodsy' buildings of the Bay Region architects and of H. H. Harris was the small beach house of Olga Zaczek at Playa del Rey (1936–8). Here are all *149* the ingredients which other architects were to use later in the forties and fifties: exposed structure, a low hipped roof, a pair of snug horizontal dormers to bring clerestory light into the house, and even vertical redwood weatherboarded walls. The Zaczek house, along with other West Coast 'woodsy' buildings, was the prototype for the popular, mildly modern and highly livable California ranch house which was mass-produced by builders and architects alike in the years after the Second World War.

The discordant roofs and overt expression of structure in these later buildings of the thirties are thus consistent with Schindler's earlier work; but the introduction of stone, with its strong overtones of tradition, permanence and even monumentality, is a new note. Again, one must posit that Schindler was simply aware of what was going on around him, and was responding to it. Even Gropius and Breuer, after all, in their

175

New England work of the late thirties, were using stone. In the
interior of the Van Dekker house (1940), or in his post-war
desert house for Maryon Toole at Palm Village (1946),
Schindler created a strong tension between the permanence of
stone and the impermanence of light wooden structure and
surfaces.

Where did Schindler stand in 1941 when the United States
entered the war? His own appraisal is contained in a letter to
Elizabeth Mock at the Museum of Modern Art (dated 10
August 1943): 'I consider myself the first and still one of the
few architects who consciously abandoned stylistic sculptural
architecture in order to develop space as a medium of art. I
believe that outside of Frank Lloyd Wright I am the only
architect in the United States who has attained a distinct local
and personal form language.' How did others see him? Hitchcock in his usual perceptive way knew what Schindler was all
about, but he didn't really approve. In an article written in
December 1940, entitled 'An Eastern Critic Looks at Western
Architecture', Hitchcock wrote:

> The case of Schindler I do not profess to understand. There
> is certainly immense vitality perhaps somewhat lacking
> among many of the best architects of the Pacific Coast. But
> this vitality seems in general to lead to arbitrary and brutal
> effects. Even his work of the last few years reminds one
> inevitably of the extreme Expressionist and Neo-Plastic work
> of the mid-twenties. Schindler's manner does not seem to
> mature. His continued reflection of the somewhat hectic
> psychological air of the region, from which all the others
> have attempted to protect themselves, still produces some-
> thing of the look of sets for a Wellsian 'film of the future'.

The Eastern architectural establishment and their professional
journals always felt ill at ease with Schindler's work, and even
in Southern California he was not enthusiastically supported.
John Entenza still published some of his buildings in *Arts and
Architecture*, but it was always with reticence.

CHAPTER THIRTEEN

The final phase

The war and the years immediately after did not mark an abrupt change in Los Angeles' pattern of growth. The numerous armaments industries (particularly aircraft) encouraged the spread of the city across even more of the Southern Californian landscape. Many of those who had come to work in these industries during the war remained as permanent residents, and many who had had their first glimpse of Arcadia while in the armed services returned as soon as they could. The first freeway had been built in the Arroyo Secco just before the war, and by the early fifties Los Angeles had, in fact and as a symbol, become the automobile city of the world.

For Southern California the late forties and the fifties mark the beginning of vast single-family housing projects, conceived on a scale that even California had not previously known. The style of these dwellings was the California ranch house, which in its best examples was a reasonable response to the Southern California environment. Though Schindler and the other local modernists had established the ranch house form, as practising architects they had little to do with the acres of middle and upper income houses built on the flat lands and the hills of the Southland. Ain, Smith and Williams, Jones and Emmons did indeed design several well-publicized housing projects, but these were inconsequential compared to what the contractors were producing. Schindler and his colleagues found it difficult to bridge the gap (much of which was public image, not architectural fact) between architecture as high art and building as low art. As operating professionals they were not, from the point of view of investors or businessmen-contractors, an appealing lot to work with.

Schindler's post-war work from 1945 until his death in 1953

has generally been considered disappointing. In 1940 one could accurately refer to the new Southern California School of Schindler, Neutra, Ain, Soriano and Harris, and there was every indication that it would continue to develop after the war with renewed vigour; but such was not the case. Their work continued at a high level, but they seem to have run out of new ideas – which were eventually to be supplied by a strong and vigorous local Miesian tradition espoused in quite different ways by Charles Eames and, later, Craig Ellwood. In the postwar period Schindler moved closer to the discordant. His buildings were no longer dominated by a single element such as his de Stijl volumes of the thirties. The atmosphere of dissonance and ambiguity, instead of being one of several means to an end, now became for him the end in itself. One entirely misses the point of his late buildings if one tries to understand them solely in the light of his work of the twenties and thirties. From outside, his post-war Laurelwood Apartments at Studio City (1948), could easily be mistaken for one of any number of contractor-investor apartments then and now being built in the Los Angeles area. What differentiates Schindler's apartments from the ordinary is what counts: his excellent siting of the complex, with its garage and automobile court separating the apartments from the street; the provision of really usable outdoor living areas; and the rich complexity of the internal spaces of each apartment.

150   Schindler's Bethlehem Church in south Los Angeles (1944) becomes perfectly understandable when seen in the context of the cardboardy world of the city. Here he employed a horizontal layered de Stijl pattern (the façade as a billboard once again), which was both simple and complex enough to attract the attention of passing cars. The open cruciform tower is readable enough to answer the question: what is the building? Having created a Christian advertising sign, Schindler successfully disposed of his spatial needs behind the billboard.

In the F. Presburger house at Studio City (1945) he again worked with the problem of the small house on a narrow urban

178

150   Bethlehem Baptist Church, Los Angeles, 1944

151   House for F. Presburger, Studio City, 1945: living room

lot. As with his own house on Kings Road, he used the entire lot: the front, set back, becomes a hedge-enclosed patio with an entrance walk on one side, while the rear of the lot is enclosed by vegetation to provide a second larger patio. While extensive fixed and movable glass walls effectively link the interior with the outdoor living spaces, the main light source is a high

151 clerestory window running the full length of the house. By the early fifties innumerable variations on the Presburger house began to appear on builders' lots throughout California.

152 The hillside house for M. Kallis at Studio City (1946) represents a strong departure from his typical pre-war de Stijl solutions. Its loose informal V-shaped plan wraps itself gently around the hill. Its battered walls are integral with the roof so that the feeling both within and without is that of a suspended platform covered by a thin tent. The central pavilion of the

153 R. Lechner house at Studio City (1948) has a similar tent-like structure. The Lechner house has not only the structure and surfaces of a typical Los Angeles builders' house, it even has the same outward form. There was just too much low art used as the medium for a high art object in the Lechner house, and in other late works such as the house for Samuel Skolnik at

154 Los Angeles (1950–52) for the professional form-oriented prophets of high art to understand them, let alone accept them.

152   House for M. Kallis, Studio City, 1946: the structure in the right foreground is the carport

153 House for R. Lechner, Studio City, 1948

154 House for Samuel Skolnik, Los Angeles, 1950–52: living room

In the last three years remaining to him, 1949–53, Schindler continued to cultivate the discordant elements even more. He branched out in one direction after another, using an ever wider range of ideas and forms. Some of these were already traditional reminiscences of his earlier de Stijl aesthetic – the Ries house at *155, 156* Los Angeles, the W. E. Tucker house at Hollywood and the remodelling of the Gonald Gordon house at Hollywood Hills, all of 1950.

These designs are purposely thinner and more suggestive of the non-permanent than anything he had produced before *157* the war. In the Adolphe Tischler house at Bel Air (1949–50), with its gabled blue corrugated fibreglass roof, he looked back *71, 34* to the Translucent House of 1927 and to the Packard house of 1924. In striking contrast to his earlier buildings, the front elevation of the Tischler house became a de Stijl stage set, expressing exactly those qualities which had so much disturbed Hitchcock in 1940. The Tischler house was difficult enough for the architectural establishment to comprehend, but the spindly

155 House for M. Ries, Los Angeles, 1950

156 House for W. E. Tucker, Hollywood, 1950

157   House for Adolphe Tischler, Bel Air, 1949–50

158 House for Ellen Janson, Hollywood, 1949

158 Ellen Janson house at Hollywood Hills (1949) was simply impossible. On its high stilts it was nothing more than a home-made tree house, suggesting that it would come down in the first wind or heavy rain storm. At least the Tischler house provided a façade which, albeit tenuously, still had some ties with classical European architecture. The Janson house tossed even this away: its sole connection was to the 'real' world of the Los Angeles builder. Hitchcock was prophetic when he wrote in 1940 that Schindler's work suggested a set for a science-fiction film; but when he wrote this Hitchcock had at least for a moment forgotten his observation of 1936 concerning Southern California: 'the combination of strict functionalism and bold symbolism in the best roadside stands provides, perhaps, the most encouraging sign for the architecture of the mid-twentieth century.' If he had remembered this he might have known what Schindler was about in 1940 and in 1953.

By the time he died in April 1953, Schindler had succeeded, but not in a self-conscious way, in bringing about a remarkable union of low and high art.

CHAPTER FOURTEEN

Schindler's place in architecture

Just where does this leave Schindler within the history of twentieth-century architecture? In his post-war letters and published comments there is an increasing bitterness towards the editors and critic-historians of modern architecture. When the Museum of Modern Art organized its first large show after the war, 'Built in USA: Post-War Architecture' (1949), Southern California was represented by Neutra, Soriano, Ain, Harris, Lloyd Wright and Eames, but not Schindler. The editors of professional journals were no longer writing to him for illustrations of his latest buildings.

The personal and professional idiosyncrasy which was present in the thirties had become even more pronounced in the late forties. Just as he could never think of changing his dress from his specially cut open-necked shirts and his sandals (not that *1* he should have), he could not discard the image of himself as the artist-architect. Like a finicky spinster, he felt increasingly that he had to be intimately involved in every aspect of design and construction. As the years went on his working drawings became more and more cursory, even sloppy; they were just enough to meet the requirements of the building departments. This left him free to improvise and design, not in the drawing office but on the site, as the building went up. Thus by 1950 his image was far closer to that of the romantic nineteenth-century artist than to the architect-engineer projecting machine symbolism into the real world of buildings.

If one still adheres to the historical concept of Giedion, Pevsner and others that the International Style was *the* style of the twentieth century, then Schindler is indeed only an 'interesting' but second-rate figure – as Pevsner once put it. Yet even within the polemical world of the Internationalists, Schindler cannot be relegated to such a lowly and insignificant

187

position: his concrete Lovell beach house is a more doctrinaire interpretation of the ideals of the International Style than Le Corbusier's Villa Savoye, Gropius' Bauhaus or Mies' Barcelona Pavilion.

However the creation of the historical tale of the International Style, and its presentation as the only logical style for the twentieth century, now stands revealed as one of the most impressive sales campaigns of recent history; with its conflicts of right and wrong it is as naïve as the classic Hollywood Cowboy and Indian film. History itself has overtaken it.

The gradual breakdown of the dominance of the International Style came from within, and occurred as early as 1949 in Charles Eames' own house in Pacific Palisades. On the surface this was a perfect product of the International Style, a volumetric box which asserted its machine origin; yet underneath it was highly subversive, for it suggested (as Schindler had done earlier) a highly potent anti-European and anti-classical mixture of high art and low art – in fact, it was more low than high. The English Brutalists of the fifties marginally sensed what the Eames house was about, the Smithsons and others trying to banish the European high art tradition from their work. Though they failed in this (classicism had too strong a hold on them), they and their apologists did succeed in bringing the issue out into the open, and thus they provided the first major hole in the seemingly impregnable armour of the International Style.

With the arrival of Charles Moore and Robert Venturi on the scene in the early sixties, the revolt was in full swing, but the final blow which toppled the International Style came not from architecture, but from the high art world of painting and sculpture. Pop art, with its 'discovery' of the juicy vitality of the 'real world' of the roadside strip, of commercial packaging and of advertising ended up playing a role close to that which Cubism, Futurism, Dadaism, Constructivism and de Stijl had played for architecture in the years before and after the First World War.

188

In looking back on the decades of the twenties and thirties, we are now able to see that the International Style was only one of several competing 'modern' points of view. Its interpretation and symbolism of the machine was impressive but it was not as intellectually valid, as Reyner Banham has shown, as that proposed by the Futurist or 'Buck Rogers' Constructivists (such as R. Buckminster Fuller), nor did it exercise the popular fascination of the Streamlined Moderne of the thirties. Since the real interest of the Internationalists was in packaging, the style also suffers appreciably (particularly in the United States) when it is compared to the run-of-the-mill contractor-built houses or commercial buildings, which were almost entirely bound up with questions of utility and economics; styling for them was packaging, nothing more.

This brings one directly back to Schindler, for his contribution was twofold. First, he transformed the symbolic image of the machine (as expressed in high art) into a form or set of forms which would have the impact and vitality of low art; the language to accomplish this was to be found in the everyday building methods used around him in Southern California. Second, he sought to transform low art (the building and the way it was put together) into high art; and for him the high art aim of architecture was the creation of space.

He understood too that the symbolic content of architecture was not static, that his symbolism should change continually and that twentieth-century symbolism to be vital, alive and meaningful must have its sources in both high and low art. His high art sources were rich and he knew them intimately – not only the International Style, but Constructivism and the spatial concepts of Loos and Wright. His low art sources were the commercial strip and the builders' houses, the various period revivals (particularly the Spanish Colonial Revival), and both phases of the Moderne. In concocting this mixture, he insisted that each of the symbols should contribute to the whole, but at the same time that each should not lose its basic identity. And with all of his passionate involvement with forms and symbols, he always retained a minimal contact with the reality of sensible planning, and the reality of cost. All of his buildings were monuments of a sort. At the moment we are only partially aware of what Schindler meant, since our intellectual and emotional ties to the concept of the International Style are still too strong. As we gradually perceive that style is packaging and nothing more, Schindler's stock will accordingly rise in the architectural market.

159 House for Schindler and Clyde Chase, Kings Road, Hollywood, 1921-2 (see above, Ills. 25-28): patio entrance to the left, patio garden to the right

A Manifesto – 1912
R. M. Schindler

1.

The cave was the original dwelling.
A hollow adobe pile was the first permanent house.
To build meant to gather and mass material, allowing it to form empty cells for human shelter.

This conception provides the basis for understanding all styles of architecture up to the twentieth century.
The aim of all architectural effort was the conquest of structural bulk by man's will for expressive form.

All architectural ideas were conditioned by the use of a plastic structural mass material.
The technique of architect and sculptor were similar.
The vault was not the result of a room conception, but of a structural system of piling masonry to support the mass enclosure. The decoration of the walls was intended to give the structural mass a plastic face.

These old problems have been solved and the styles are dead.

Our efficient way of using materials eliminated the plastic structural mass.
The contemporary architect conceives the 'room' and forms it with ceiling and wall slabs.

The architectural design concerns itself with 'space' as its raw material and with the articulated room as its product.

Because of the lack of a plastic mass the shape of the inner room defines the exterior of the building. Therefore the early primitive product of this new development is the 'box-shaped' house.

The architect has finally discovered the medium of his art: S P A C E.

A new architectural problem has been born. Its infancy is being shielded as always by emphasizing functional advantages.

2.

The first house was a shelter.
Its primary attribute was stability.
Therefore its structural features were paramount.
All architectural styles up to the twentieth century were functional.

Architectural forms symbolized the structural functions of the building material.
The final step in this development was the architectural solution of the steel skeleton: Its framework is no longer a symbol, it has become form itself.

The twentieth century is the first to abandon construction as a source for architectural form through the introduction of reinforced concrete.

The structural problem has been reduced to an equation. The approved stress diagram eliminates the need to emphasize the stability of the construction.

Modern man pays no attention to structural members.
There are no more columns with base, shaft and cap, no more wall masses with foundation course and cornice.
He sees the daring of the cantilever, the freedom of the wide span, the space-forming surfaces of thin wall screens.

Structural styles are obsolete.
Functionalism is a hollow slogan used to lead the conservative stylist to exploit contemporary techniques.

3.

Monumentality is the mark of power.
The first master was the tyrant.
He symbolized his power over the human
mass by his control over matter.
The power symbol of primitive culture was
confined to the defeat of two simple re-
sistances of matter: gravity and cohesion.

Monumentality became apparent
in proportion to the human mass
displacement effort.
Man cowers before an early might.

Today a different power is asking for
its monument.
The mind destroyed the power of the tyrant.
The machine has become the ripe symbol for
man's control over nature's forces.
Our mathematical victory over structural
stresses eliminates them as a source of
art forms.
The new monumentality of space
will symbolize the limitless power
of the human mind.
Man trembles facing the universe.

4.

The feeling of security of our ancestor
came in the seclusion and confinement of
his cave.

The same feeling of security was the aim of
the medieval city plan which crowded

the largest possible number of
defenders inside the smallest ring
of walls and bastions.
The peasant's hut comforts him by an
atmosphere in violent contrast to
his enemy: the out of doors.

Rooms that are designed to recall such
feelings of security out of our past
are acclaimed as 'comfortable and
cozy'.

The man of the future does not try to
escape the elements.
He will rule them.

His home is no more a timid retreat:
The earth has become his home.

The concepts 'comfortable' and 'home'
change their meaning.
Atavistic security feelings fail to
recommend conventional designs.

The comfort of the dwelling lies in its
complete control of:
space, climate, light, mood,
within its confines.

The modern dwelling will not freeze
temporary whims of owner or
designer into permanent tiresome
features.

It will be a quiet, flexible background
for a harmonious life.

Space Architecture – 1934
R. M. Schindler

Anybody who reads about modern architecture in current publications comes constantly upon the reiteration of how important it is for the modern architect to deal with 'space'. However, if one analyses the various pronunciamentos issued by the groups or individuals who want to lead the modern architectural movement, one does not find any real grasp of the space problem.

In the summer of 1911, sitting in one of the earthbound peasant cottages on top of a mountain pass in Styria, a sudden realization of the meaning of space in architecture came to me. Here was the house, its heavy walls built of the stone of the mountain, plastered over by groping hands – in feeling and material nothing but an artificial reproduction of one of the many caverns in the mountain-side. I saw that essentially all architecture of the past, whether Egyptian or Roman, was nothing but the work of a sculptor dealing with abstract forms. The architect's attempt really was – to gather and pile up masses of building material, leaving empty hollows for human use. His many efforts at form-giving resolved themselves continuously into carving and decorating the surface layers of his mass-pile. The room itself was a by-product. The vault was not invented as a room-form, but as primarily a scheme to keep the masses hovering. The architectural treatment of the inner room confined itself to the sculptural carving of the four walls and ceiling, shaping them into separate faces of the surrounding pile of sculptural mass.

And although improved technique has constantly reduced the actual bulk of this structural pile, essentially the architect was still concerned with its sculptural treatment. All conventional architecture of the occident, including all historical styles, was nothing but sculpture.

And, stooping through the doorway of the bulky, spreading house, I looked up into the sunny sky. Here I saw the real medium of architecture – SPACE. A new medium as far as human history goes. Only primitive uncertain gropings for its possibilities can be found in historical buildings. Even the gothic builder merely caught it between his sculptured pillars without attempting to use it consciously as a medium of his art.

'Architecture' is being born in our time. In all really modern buildings the attitude of the architect is fundamentally different from the one of the sculptor and the one of his brother, the conventional architect. He is not primarily concerned with the body of the structure and its sculptural possibilities. His one concern is the creation of space forms – dealing with a new medium as rich and unlimited in possibilities of expression as any of the other media of art: color, sound, mass, etc.

This gives us a new understanding of the task of modern architecture. Its experiments serve to develop a new language, a vocabulary and syntax of space. Only as far as the various schools help us in that direction can they be considered significant.

Shortly after my revelation in the mountains, a librarian in Vienna handed me a portfolio – the work of Frank Lloyd Wright. Immediately

I realized – here was a man who had taken hold of this new medium. Here was 'space architecture'. It was not any more the questions of moldings, caps and finials – here was space forms in meaningful shapes and relations. Here was the first architect. And the timeless importance of Wright lies especially in these first houses. I feel that in his later work he has again become sculptural. He tries to weave his buildings into the character of the locality through sculptural forms. The hotel in Tokio seems the play of a virtuoso with traditional oriental motives, rather than the product of a direct impregnation by the nature of the locale. And although as an artist far above most of his contemporaries, this somewhat relates his later work to the 'Modernistic School.'

In the main the work which is generally called 'modernistic' is an architectural backwash of the several movements of modern art in Europe, such as futurism, cubism, etc. These buildings try to achieve an up-to-date city character by a play with highly-conventionalized contrasting sculptural forms. Instead of conceiving the building as a frame which will help to create the life of the future, they limit themselves, like a painting or a piece of music, to an expression of the present with all its interesting short-comings. And it is in this way that the buildings of the World's Fair in Chicago have to be understood. Architecturally they are the last outcry of the chaos of the recent past, unfortunately without any attempt at opening a way toward a better architectural future.

The sub-conscious realization that architecture in its old sculptural form has died as an art, leads to an attitude characteristic of our age. Blind to the growth of a new art dealing with a new medium (space) in their midst, the 'Functionalists' ask us to dismiss architecture as an art altogether. They want to build as the engineer does, producing 'types' without other meaning but that of function. They limit themselves entirely to the problems of civilization – that is the struggle to adapt our surrounding to our limitations. They forget that architecture as an art may have the much more important meaning of serving as a cultural agent – stimulating and fulfilling the urge for growth and extension of our own selves.

To make matters worse and public attention more concentrated, a group of functionalists have given their breed a name: International Style. Problems of form as such are completely dismissed. The manufacturer (influenced by considerations of available equipment, competition, labor rules, profit, and personal inertia, etc.) is the god who furnishes 'form' ready-made. The classical code of set forms for columns, architraves and cornices, is replaced by [a] stereotyped vocabulary of steel columns, horizontal parapets, and corner windows, all to be used equally both in the jungles and on the glaciers.

The ideal of perfection of the new sloganists is the machine – without regard for the fact that the present machine is a crude collection of working parts, far from being an organism. Endlessly we are being shown photographs of the present automobiles as an example of formal machine perfection, forgetting that what we see in looking at a modern automobile is not a 'machine'. The sheet-metal hood with which its designer covers the working parts is only slightly functional. It is very definitely nationally characterized, subject to fashion, and bound by a tradition as relentless as the one which defines our clothes. What is still more important, the automobile, and for that matter all machines, are essentially one-dimensional, whereas the house as an *organism* in direct relation with our lives must be of four dimensions.

Most of the buildings which Corbusier and his followers offer us as 'machines to live in', equipped with various 'machines to sit and sleep on', have not even reached the state of development of our present machines. They are crude 'contraptions' to serve a purpose. The man who brings such machines into his living-room is on the same level of primitive development as the farmer who keeps cows and pigs in his house. Mere instruments of production can never serve as a frame for life. Especially the creaks and jags of our crude machine age must necessarily force us to protect our human qualities in homes contrasting most intensely with the factory.

The factory must remain our servant. And if a 'Machine-Made House' shall ever emerge from it, it will have to meet the requirements of our imagination and not be merely a result of present production methods. The work of Mr. Buckminster-Fuller in propagating the tremendous possibilities which the use of our technique of production may have for building construction, is invaluable. If he creates his Dymaxion house, however, entirely from the viewpoint of facile manufacture, letting all considerations of 'what' take care of themselves, he is putting the cart before the horse. The space architect has primarily a vision of a future life in a future house. And with the clearing of that vision the necessary technique for its realization will undoubtedly develop. Although Mr Buckminster-Fuller realizes the coming importance of space-considerations in architecture, his Dymaxion house is not a 'space creation'. However 'ephemeral', to use his own term, it may be, it is born of a sculptural conception. Its structural scheme is akin to the one of the tree, and although its branches and members may try to.wed it to space by the tenderest interlockings, the 'room' they enclose is not an aimful space conception but a by-product without architectural meaning.

Modern architecture can not be developed by changing slogans. It is not in the hands of the engineer, the efficiency expert, the machinist or the economist. It is developing in the minds of the artists who can grasp 'space' and 'space forms' as a new medium for human expression. The development of this new language is going on amongst us, unconsciously in most cases, partly realized in some. It is not merely the birth of a new style, or a new version of the old play with sculptural forms, but the subjection of a new medium to serve as a vehicle for human expression.

(*Dune Forum*, February 1934)

Major buildings and projects

Within each year, works are listed as far as possible in chronological order. Projects appear in *italic* type.

1912 *Hotel Rong, Vienna*
Hunting lodge, Vienna
Clubhouse for Actors, 'Österreichischen Bühnenverein' (for Hans Mayr and Theodor Mayer), 6 Dorotheergasse, Vienna. Still standing and in good condition
Crematorium and chapel, 'Totenfeld für eine 5 mill. Stadt', Vienna; 1912–13

1914 *Summer house, near Vienna*
Neighbourhood centre, Chicago (Chicago Architectural Club competition)

1915 *Eleven-storey hotel, Chicago (for Ottenheimer, Stern and Reichert)*
Bar, Chicago (for Ottenheimer, Stern and Reichert); c. 1915
House for T. P. Martin, Taos, N.M.
Homer Emunim Temple and School, Chicago (for Ottenheimer, Stern and Reichert); 1915–16

1916 *Store front, Chicago (for Ottenheimer, Stern and Reichert)*
Central administration building, Chicago (for Ottenheimer, Stern and Reichert); c. 1916
Women's club, Chicago
Remodelling of house for J. B. Lee, street address unknown, Maywood, Ill. Altered
Hampden Club (?), Chicago (for Ottenheimer, Stern and Reichert)

1917 *Melrose Public Park, Melrose, Ill.*
'Log House', location not given; 1916–17

Buena Shore Club, Chicago (for Ottenheimer, Stern and Reichert); 1917–18. Destroyed
Three-room house, Oak Park, Ill.

1918 *Children's Corner, Chicago Art Institute, Chicago*

1919 *One-room apartments, Chicago (for Ottenheimer, Stern and Reichert)*
Memorial Community Center, no street address given, Wenatchee, Wash. (for Frank Lloyd Wright). Replanned
House for C. E. Staley, no street address given, Waukegan, Ill. (for Frank Lloyd Wright)
J. P. Shampay house, no street address given, Chicago (for Frank Lloyd Wright)
Workmen's Colony of 'Monolith Homes' (for Frank Lloyd Wright)

1920 *Temporary house for J. B. Irving, Wilmette, Ill. (for Frank Lloyd Wright)*
Actors' Abode, apartment house for actors, for Miss A. Barnsdall, Olive Hill, Los Angeles (for Frank Lloyd Wright)
Director's house for Miss A. Barnsdall, Olive Hill, corner of Hollywood Blvd and Vermont Ave., Los Angeles (for Frank Lloyd Wright). Remodelled, in poor condition
Terrace stores for Miss A. Barnsdall, Olive Hill, Los Angeles (for Frank Lloyd Wright)

Oleanders, house for Miss A. Barnsdall, Olive Hill, Los Angeles (for Frank Lloyd Wright). Destroyed
Free Public Library, Bergen Branch, Jersey City, N.J. (competition)
Double house, industrial housing (for Los Angeles)

1921 *Walt Whitman School, Los Angeles*
First scheme for R. M. Schindler house, Hollywood
Double house for R. M. Schindler and Clyde Chase, 833 N. Kings Rd, Hollywood; 1921–2. Some remodelling, in good condition
Bungalow court for J. Korsen, Los Angeles
Sketch for an apartment building for Los Angeles
'The Playmart', skyscraper of black glass and aluminium, Los Angeles

1922 Beauty salon for Helena Rubinstein, Los Angeles. Destroyed
House for C. P. Lowes, Eagle Rock (for Frank Lloyd Wright)
Apartment buildings for I. Binder and H. Gross, Soto St., Los Angeles. Remodelled
Duplexes and small apartments for O. S. Floren, Hollywood (*1* NE corner of Harper and Romaine; *2* NW corner of La Jolla and Romaine; *3* 5075 Romaine); 1922–5. All extensively remodelled
Duplex for Mrs A. M. Burrell, Hollywood. Destroyed
Double dwelling for F. Henderson, Los Angeles. Destroyed
Remodelling of apartment building for B. Caplan and others, Los Angeles. Destroyed
Duplex for Mrs E. E. Lacey, 830–832 Laguna Ave., Los Angeles. Remodelled

House for W. E. Kent, Los Angeles
Bungalow for P. L. Mix, Los Angeles
House for Mrs L. Davies, Los Angeles; c. 1922–4
House for M. P. Campbell, Los Angeles
House for W. G. Duncan, Los Angeles
House for Mrs R. Lindquist, Hollywood
Photographic studio for Miss V. Baker, Los Angeles; 1922 and 1924. Destroyed
Apartment building for E. Temple, Hollywood
Cabin for P. Popenoe, Coachella; 1922 and 1924. Destroyed
House for Mrs A. M. Burrell
First drawings for beach house for Dr P. M. Lovell, Newport Beach

1923 Apartment building for S. Friedman and A. Kopley, 115 N. Soto St., Los Angeles. Remodelled
Duplex for Mrs A. L. Paine, 1024 Havenhurst Ave., Los Angeles. Remodelled
House for Dr P. M. Lovell, Hollywood
House for C. P. Lowes, Eagle Rock (four different schemes). Destroyed
Alterations to Hotel Wind and Sea, La Jolla, for T. E. Snell
House for Mrs C. Warne, Los Angeles
House for Mrs M. D. Baker, Hollywood
New art room for the Hollywood Public Library, Hollywood (with Douglas Donaldson)
Physical education club lodge for Topanga Ranch, Topanga Canyon, Los Angeles County
Store and hotel building for J. E. Neville, Hollywood
Remodelling and additions to Helena Rubinstein house, no street address given, Greenwich, Conn.

Beach studio (and store) for E. Leswin and H. Leepa, Castel La Mar. Destroyed
Pueblo Ribera community for W. L. Lloyd, 230 Gravilla St., La Jolla. Remodelled, but basic form intact
House for Mrs W. Baker, Hollywood
Apartment building for Mrs C. Kruetzer, 1620–1626 N. Gower St., Los Angeles. Remodelled
'Four-Flat' building, 5427 Harold Way, Los Angeles. Remodelled

1924 *Sketch for a house in the desert for P. Popinoff, Coachella; c. 1924?*
Vacation house for Dr P. M. Lovell, Wrightwood. Destroyed
'Workmen's Colony', industrial housing scheme for Gould, Bandini
Remodelling of apartment building for Mrs F. Braun, 6092 Selma Ave., Los Angeles. Remodelled
House for J. C. Packard, 931 N. Gainsborough Dr., South Pasadena. Many remodellings
The Peoples Bank, Los Angeles
House for A. Plotkin, Los Angeles
Garden wall and landscaping for Miss A. Barnsdall, Olive Hill, Los Angeles. Still extant
House for H. Levin, 2376 Dundee Pl., Los Angeles (Architectural Group for Industry and Commerce); 1924–33. In good condition
Nurembega Heights Hotel, Burbank
Harriman Colony, location not given; 1924–5
House for E. J. Gibling, Los Angeles. Destroyed

1925 Remodelling of Director's house and main residence for Miss A. Barnsdall, Olive Hill, Los Angeles
Hotel and bungalow community for P. Popinoff, Coachella; c. 1925

House for J. E. Howe, 2422 Silver Ridge Ave., Los Angeles. Hipped roof added
First scheme for resort hotel, 'Hotel Elsinore', Elsinore (with A. R. Brandner and R. J. Neutra)
Wading pool and pergola for Miss A. Barnsdall, Olive Hill, Hollywood Blvd and Edgemont St., Los Angeles. Intact
Photographic studio for Ambassador Hotel, Los Angeles
Bedroom for Dr P. M. Lovell, Los Angeles. No longer extant
Ranch house for Dr P. M. Lovell, Fallbrook. Destroyed
Furniture for the children's workshop, for Dr P. M. Lovell, Los Angeles
Tea room for Mrs O'Sullivan and Miss B. Kent, Los Angeles. Destroyed
Brudin house, El Monte
Apartment building for S. Breacher, Los Angeles. Destroyed
Beach house for Dr P. M. Lovell, 1242 Ocean Ave., Newport Beach; 1925–6. Intact
Ranch house for C. Park, Fallbrook. Destroyed

1926 Remodelling of house for F. M. Weiner, 1120 Court St., Los Angeles
House for Briggs, Newport Beach
Sketch for an exhibition room, Berkeley; c. 1926
Studio for J. Morgenthau, Palm Springs
House for Martec, Los Angeles, 1926–8
House for C. B. Price, Los Angeles, c. 1926–8
Leah-Ruth Shop, Long Beach (AGIC). Destroyed
Haines Health Food Store, Los Angeles. Destroyed
Beach house for D. Lovell, Newport Beach

Manola Court, apartment building for H. Sachs, 1811–1813 Edgecliff Dr., Los Angeles; 1926–40. In good condition
House for Mrs K. Sorg, 600 S. Putney Ave., San Gabriel. Remodelled
League of Nations Building (international competition, with R.J. Neutra)
Apartments for M. Brown, Hollywood
Hain house, Los Angeles (AGIC)
Apartment buildings for Hennessey brothers, Los Angeles; c. 1926
Apartment building for Levy, Los Angeles

1927 Furniture for S. Freeman house, 1695 Glencoe Way, Hollywood
Second scheme for resort hotel, 'Hotel Elsinore', Elsinore (AGIC, with A. R. Brandner)
Five-storey apartment building for J.H. Miller, Los Angeles (AGIC)
Four-storey class C apartment building, Pasadena (AGIC)
Aesop's Chest and Nosegay Store, Los Angeles. Destroyed
Temporary outdoor poster exhibition pavilion for Miss A. Barnsdall, Olive Hill, Los Angeles
Garden Apartments, Los Angeles (AGIC)
Alternate scheme for five-storey apartment house for J.H. Miller, Los Angeles (AGIC)
Falcon Flyers Country Club, near Wasco, Kern County (AGIC), c. 1927–8
Oil mill for J. Napolitano, 676 Clover St., Los Angeles (AGIC)
Remodelling of house for J. E. Richardson, 8272 Marmont Way, Los Angeles (AGIC)
House for T. Zaczek, Los Angeles (AGIC)

Translucent House for Miss A. Barnsdall, Palos Verdes
Amusement centre, garage and stores, Los Angeles (AGIC), c. 1927

1928 *Twin Harbor community, Catalina Island (AGIC)*
House for Slemons, Los Angeles
Art Gallery, Lake Merritt, Oakland (AGIC)
House for H. Braxton, Venice, Calif. An identical project at the same address reappears in 1930 under the name of V.B. Shore
Remodelling of Oleanders, house for Miss A. Barnsdall, Olive Hill, Los Angeles. Destroyed
The Golden Pyramid, also called The Pyramid of Gold, Los Angeles
Summer house for C.H. Wolfe, no street address given, Avalon, Catalina Island. In good condition
Setting for *Soul of Raphael*, for Opera and Drama Guild, at Trinity Auditorium, Los Angeles
Braxton Gallery, Hollywood. Destroyed
House for D. Grokowsky, 816 Bonita Dr., South Pasadena. Remodelled, but basic form intact

1929 *Hotel, Hollywood (AGIC)*
Remodelling of house for H. D. Diffen, Avalon, Catalina Island
Addition of studio, workroom, and garage for Vorkapic, Beverly Hills
Coffee shop for hotel, Tucson (for Tucson Holding Company)
Wolfe School of Costume Designing, Los Angeles. Destroyed
Satyre Bookshop, Los Angeles. Destroyed
Studio for an artist (location not given)
Lavana Studio Building for Sieburt, Los Angeles

Automobile show room, Lincoln Garage Building, Beverly Hills (with H. Sachs). Destroyed

Cabin for W. Lingenbrink, Calabasas. Destroyed

Store front for J.J. Newberry, Los Angeles (with H. Sachs)

Paradise Resort, Ontario

Cabin No. 1 at Park Moderne, Blackbird Way, Woodland Hills. Remodelled, but basic form intact

Effie Dean Café, Los Angeles (AGIC)

Apartment building for Frankel, Los Angeles

Remodelling of house for Vorkapic, 2100 Benedict Canyon, Beverly Hills. Remodelled

Scheme for an Easter puppet show, Los Angeles; c. 1929

1930 *Market for J.M. Cohan, Los Angeles (AGIC)*

Exposition buildings and park, Los Angeles

Remodelling of house and furniture for Gisela (Mrs A.) Bennati, Los Angeles. Not fully carried out

Store building for E. George and S. Freeman, Los Angeles; 1930–31

House for R.F. Elliot, 4237 Newdale Dr., Los Angeles. In good condition

Hotel and subdivision for G.L. Wing, Banning (AGIC)

Nobby Knit Store, Los Angeles; c. 1930

Desert house for Kopenlanoff, Palm Springs

Subdivision scheme for Kopenlanoff, Palm Springs (AGIC)

Auditorium and civic centre, Richmond (competition; AGIC)

1931 Apartment house for Mrs Cherry, 3910 S. Walton St., Los Angeles

Apartment for Hollywood Riviera Building Association, Hollywood

Remodelling of house for R. Marx, 1557 N. Courtney Ave., Los Angeles

Two-car garage for the residence of G. Stojano, 8501 Dahlia St., Los Angeles. In good condition

Highway bungalow hotels, no location given (AGIC)

First scheme for house for W.E. Oliver, Los Angeles

House for H.N. Von Koerber, 408 Monte d'Oro, Hollywood Riviera, Torrance

The Embassy Restaurant and Arcade, Los Angeles

1932 Speculative house No. 2, Park Moderne, Blackbird Way, Woodland Hills

House for F. Hanna, Los Angeles; c. 1932

House for Miss H. Lierd and Miss E. Todd, Los Angeles

House for J. Veissi, Hollywood; c. 1932–6

Bread Pit Stores, Los Angeles; 1932–3. Destroyed

Retail store and olive oil bath, Lindsay; 1932 and 1935

Prototype service station for Standard Oil Company

Donnell's Desert Hotel, Twentynine Palms

Automobile store for Brown, Smith and Moore, Los Angeles

Show windows for the May Co., Los Angeles (with A.R. Brandner and B.P. Paradise)

Sardi's Restaurant No. 1, Hollywood; 1932–4. Destroyed

Lindy' Restaurant No. 1, Hollywood; 1932–4. Destroyed

1933 *'Schindler Shelters' (schemes for concrete and wood frame single-family houses)*

Dance hall for O. K. Farr, Denver
House for W. E. Oliver, 2236
Micheltorena St., Los Angeles. In
good condition
*Prototype service stations for Union Oil
Company, Los Angeles*
*Two schemes for house for E. Locke,
Los Angeles*
Remodelling and living-room furni-
ture for Perstein, 111 Tamalpais
Rd, Berkeley
The Oven, retail bakery for
Frederick, Los Angeles. Destroyed
*Dance-restaurant for S. Grauman, Los
Angeles*
*First concept for panel post construction
(others in 1936 and 1938)*

1934 Mountain cabin for Gisela (Mrs A.)
Bennati, no street address given,
Lake Arrowhead; 1934–7. In good
condition
House for J. J. Buck, 8th and Genesee
Sts, Los Angeles. In good condi-
tion
*Remodelling of house for Dondo,
583 Tamalpais Rd, Berkeley*
House for Haines, 5112 Alishia Dr.,
Dana Point; 1934–5. In good
condition
Remodelling and furniture for house
of H. R. King, 10354 La Grange,
Westwood
Remodelling of house for Mrs M.
Kipp, 1773 Griffith Park Blvd,
Los Angeles; 1934 and 1937
Remodelling and furniture for house
of E. Pavaroff, 1641 N. Crescent
Heights Blvd, Los Angeles
House for Ransom, Palm Springs
Remodelling of house for Mrs G.
Rheingold, 8730 Sunset Blvd,
Los Angeles
House at Leimert Park, Los Angeles
*Service station for Mrs Nerenbaum,
no location given*

House for Miss E. Van Patten, 2320
Moreno Dr., Los Angeles; 1934–
5. In good condition

1935 Remodelling of house for L. Stander,
2006 La Brea Terrace, Hollywood
Apartments for L. Stander, Los Angeles
*Mountain cabins and hospital for P. S.
O'Reilly*
House for P. Heraty, Los Angeles
House for R. G. Walker, 2100
Kenilworth Ave., Los Angeles;
1935–6. In good condition
*First Baptist Church of Hollywood,
Hollywood*
Double house for J. DeKeyser, 1911
Highland Ave., Hollywood. In
good condition
*Two schemes for a house for M. Shep,
Los Angeles*
*House for W. J. Delahoyde, Los
Angeles*
Remodelling of house for L. Stander,
Los Angeles
*Two schemes for M. Geggie house,
Pasadena; 1935–6*
*First sketch for main house and secon-
dary house for Miss V. McAlmon,
2721 Waverly Dr., Los Angeles*

1936 Beach house for Miss O. Zaczek,
114 Ellen Ave., Playa Del Rey;
1936–8. In good condition
House for C. C. Fitzpatrick, 8078
Woodrow Wilson Dr., Holly-
wood Hills. In good condition
Sunset Medical Buildings for A.
Garland, 6642 Sunset Blvd.,
Hollywood. Extensively re-
modelled
*Two schemes for a house for W.
Jacobs, Beverly Glen*
Beach house for A. Kaun, 112
Western Dr., Richmond. Re-
modelled
House for E. Mack, Hollywood

House for Schuettner, Los Angeles
Modern Creators Store Building, corner of Holloway Dr. and Palm Ave., Hollywood; 1936–8. Extensively remodelled
Remodelling of house for S. Seligson, 1671 Orange Grove Dr., Los Angeles
Remodelling and furniture for Seff house, address unknown, Los Angeles
House for Mrs F. Miller (for Mrs R. Shep), Los Angeles
House for Warshaw (client not traced), Los Angeles
Craft workshop for M. Kipp, Los Angeles. Destroyed
House for E. Pavaroff, Beverly Hills
House for E. Mack, Los Angeles
Furniture for Chayes, Los Angeles
House for Mrs B. Berkoff, Los Angeles; 1936–7
Main house and secondary house for Miss V. McAlmon, 2721 Waverly Dr., Los Angeles. In good condition

1937 Store buildings for W. Lingenbrink, 8750 Holloway Dr., Hollywood. Additions in 1946
House No. 2 for C. P. Lowes, Eagle Rock. Destroyed
House for H. Rodakiewicz, 9121 Alto Cedro Dr., Los Angeles. In good condition
Beach colony for A. E. Rose, no location given. Identical with Cabania City project, Santa Monica
Remodelling of house and furniture for H. Warren, 1115 N. Beverly Dr., Hollywood Hills
Beach house for R. R. Ryan, no location given
House for N. Renisoff, Los Angeles

1938 Remodelling of house for P. Yates, 1735 Micheltorena St., Los Angeles. In good condition
Apartment building for A. L. Bubeshko, 2036 Griffith Park Blvd, Los Angeles; later addition, 1941. In good condition
Apartment building for I. Rosenthal, Los Angeles
Studio-house for Mrs A. Sharpless, Los Angeles
Studio-house for Mrs M. Southall, 1855 Park Ave., Los Angeles. In good condition
House for A. Timme, Los Angeles
House for S. N. Westby, 1805 Maltman Ave., Los Angeles. In good condition
House for G. C. Wilson, 2090 Redcliff St., Los Angeles. In good condition
House for H. Wolff, Jr., 4008 Sunnyslope Ave., Studio City. In good condition
Speculative house No. 3, Park Moderne, Woodland Hills. Destroyed
House for K. Francis, Hollywood Hills
House for F. Hanna, Los Angeles
Photographic shop for Morgan, Hollywood
House for R. Shep, Los Angeles. Other schemes in 1935 and 1936
House (including apartments) for Burke, Newport Beach
House for E. Djey and M. Aldrich, Los Angeles
Interior of Lockheed 27, 24-passenger airplane, two alternate schemes (with H. Sachs)

1939 Apartment building for S. T. Falk, 3631 Carnation Ave., Los Angeles. In good condition

Remodelling of house for Good-
man, 2149 Casitas Ave., Altadena
Stores for W. Lingenbrink, 12560
Ventura Blvd, Studio City; later
stores designed and built in 1940,
1941, and 1942. Remodelled
House for A. Bissiri, Los Angeles
*House for T. Balkany, North Holly-
wood*
The Hub Office Building, Los Angeles
Apartment building for Mrs P.
Mackey, 1137 S. Cochran Ave.,
Los Angeles. In good condition
Remodelling of house for Miss
A. M. Wong, address unknown,
Santa Monica

1940 House for G. Droste, 2035 Kenil-
worth Ave., Los Angeles. In
good condition
House for S. Goodwin, 3807
Reklaw Dr., Studio City. Some
remodelling
Remodelling and furniture for house
of G. H. Hodel, 1800 Huntington
Dr., San Marino
House for J. Rodriguez, Glendale
Lapotka Apartments, Los Angeles
Three speculative houses, 423, 429
and 433 Ellis Ave., Inglewood
(with E. Richard Lind); c. 1940
House for A. Van Dekker, 5230
Penfield Ave. (to the rear of
property), Canoga Park. In good
condition
House for A. M. Sax, Los Angeles
House for J. Strader, North Hollywood
*House for N. M. Taylor, South
Pasadena*

1941 House for J. Rodriguez, 1845 Nio-
drara Dr., Glendale
House for B. Carre, Los Angeles
House for Hartigan, Hollywood Park
Studio-house for H. Hiler, Holly-
wood. Destroyed

House for W. Byers, Van Nuys
House for E. J. Gibling, Los Angeles
House for J. Druckman, 2764 Out-
post Dr., Los Angeles. Some re-
modelling
Karz Apartments, Los Angeles
House for M. Periere, Los Angeles

1942 Automobile trailer
Remodelling of house for Albers,
2781 Outpost Dr., Los Angeles
House for R. L. Harris, Los Angeles.
Destroyed
Officers' Club, Palm Springs
Remodelling of ranch house 'Pen
Oaks', for J. Pennington, Thou-
sand Oaks, Camarillo. In good
condition
*Apartment building for Mrs S. T.
Falk, Los Angeles; 3 alternate
schemes*

1943 Remodelling of house for Langley,
841 Stone Canyon, Brentwood
*Remodelling of house for C. Marker,
Los Angeles*
House for A. Fisher, Los Angeles
Remodelling of house for K.
Howenstein, South Pasadena

1944 Bethlehem Baptist Church, 4900
S. Compton Ave., Los Angeles. In
good condition
*Remodelling of Hollywood Women's
Club, Los Angeles*
Remodelling of house for Litt,
3050 Menlo, Glendale
Remodelling of house for Mrs H.
Nickerson, 681 Norton St., Los
Angeles
Remodelling of duplex for C. Rosoff,
6000–6002 La Prada Park, Los
Angeles
*Remodelling of apartment for K. K.
Thomasset, Los Angeles*

Remodelling of house for W. A. Starkey, 2330 Merrywood, Los Angeles
Addition of studio to house for R. Sabsay, Los Angeles

1945 *House for D. M. H. Braden, North Hollywood*
House for M. Compinsky, Burbank
House for J. G. Gold, 3758 Reklaw Dr., Los Angeles. Some remodelling
Medical Arts Building, 12307 Ventura Blvd, Studio City. Some remodelling
House for F. Presburger, 4255 Agnes Ave., Studio City. Some remodelling
House for R. Roth, 3624 Buena Park Dr., North Hollywood. Some remodelling
House for H. Schick, North Hollywood
Hotel for L. Anson, no location given

1946 House for F. Daugherty, 4635 Louise Ave., Encino. Some remodelling
Kermin Medical Building, Los Angeles
Desert house for M. Toole, Palm Village, no street address given. In good condition
House for M. Kallis, 3580 Multiview Dr., Studio City. In good condition
Remodelling of house for C. E. Harvey, Los Angeles
House for Mrs F. Howatt, Laguna Beach
Lord Leigh Showroom and Office (remodelling of interior of existing building), 847 S. Santee, Los Angeles
Redesdale Avenue Apartments, Los Angeles
House for R. M. Spangler, Los Angeles
Pottery works for Miss P. West, Los Angeles. Destroyed

Medical office for E. Tietz (remodelling of interior of existing building), Los Angeles; 1946–9. Destroyed
House for J. L. Armon, 470 W. Avenue 43, Los Angeles; 1946–9. In good condition
Apartments for L. Gallagher, Los Angeles

1947 *House for M. Mangaldas, Los Angeles*
Remodelling of house for Courcio, Los Angeles
Rest home for H. Schick and Associates, Los Angeles
Duplex for F. Virginia, Los Angeles
House for T. Trumbo, Los Angeles
House for A. Borisof, Los Angeles
Theoretical space development

1948 House for R. Lechner, 11606 Amanda Dr., Studio City. Some remodelling
Motel for H. Schick and Associates, Los Angeles
House for E. J. Gibling, Los Angeles. *See also 1941*
Apartment building for P. P. Ott, Beverly Hills
Laurelwood Apartments, 11833 Laurelwood Dr., Studio City. In good condition
House for M. Sax, Los Angeles
Drive-in theatre, Los Angeles (?)

1949 *Washington Palace Motel for H. Schick, Los Angeles*
House for A. Tischler, 175 Greenfield Ave., Bel Air; 1949–50. In good condition
House for Miss E. Janson, 8704 Skyline Dr., Hollywood Hills. Remodelled
Beverly Hills penthouse, Beverly Hills
House for L. Blembel, Hollywood

Remodelling of house for B. Myers, 2040 Oakstone Way, Hollywood
House for Miss B. Inaya, Beverly Hills; c. 1949–50

1950 House for W. E. Tucker, 8010 Fareholm Dr., Hollywood. Some remodelling
House for M. Ries, 1404 Miller Dr., Los Angeles; 1950–51. Some remodelling
Remodelling of house for D. Gordon, 6853 Pacific View Dr., Hollywood Hills. In good condition
Building for Kaynor Manufacturing Company, 811 E. 17th St., Los Angeles
Additions to beach house for Mrs O. Zaczek, Playa Del Rey

House for R. Erlik, 1757 Curson Ave., Hollywood; 1950–51. Some remodelling
House for S. Skolnik, 2567 Glendower Ave., Los Angeles; 1950–52. In good condition

1952 *Apartment, Los Angeles*
House for O. Elmer, Hollywood
Remodelling of existing house into duplex for Esther McCoy (Tobey), 2434 Beverly Blvd, Santa Monica. Never fully completed
House for Schlesinger, 1901 Myra Ave., Los Angeles. In good condition

1953 Remodelling of house for S. Marks, 1052 Manzanita St., Los Angeles

Bibliography

By R. M. Schindler

'Modern Architecture: A Program' (unpublished manuscript), Vienna 1912
'Notes on Architecture' (unpublished manuscript), Chicago 1914–19
'About Architecture' (unpublished lecture), Hollywood 1921
'Who Will Save Hollywood?' *Holly Leaves* (Hollywood), 3 November 1922, p. 32
'Ventilation' ('Care of the Body'), *Los Angeles Times* Sunday magazine section, 14 March 1926, pp. 25–6
'Plumbing and Health' ('Care of the Body'), *Los Angeles Times* Sunday magazine section, 21 March 1926, pp. 25–6
'About Heating' ('Care of the Body'), *Los Angeles Times* Sunday magazine section, 28 March 1926, pp. 24–5
'About Lighting' ('Care of the Body'), *Los Angeles Times* Sunday magazine section, 7 April 1926, pp. 30–31
'About Furniture' ('Care of the Body'), *Los Angeles Times* Sunday magazine section, 14 April 1926, pp. 26–7
'Shelter or Playground' ('Care of the Body'), *Los Angeles Times* Sunday magazine section, 21 April 1926, pp. 26–7
Civic Center Design for Richmond, California, City Planning Commission for Richmond, 15 November 1930

'A Cooperation Dwelling', *T-Square* (Philadelphia), vol. 2, no. 2, February 1932, pp. 20–21

'Points of View – Contra', *Southwest Review* (Austin and Dallas, Texas), vol. 17, Spring 1932, pp. 353–4

'Space Architecture', *Dune Forum* (Oceano, Calif.), February 1934, pp. 44–6

'Space Architecture' (unpublished manuscript), September 1934

'Space Architecture', *California Arts and Architecture* (San Francisco), vol. 47, January 1935, pp. 18–19

'Furniture and the Modern House: A Theory of Interior Design', *Architect and Engineer* (San Francisco), vol. 123, December 1935, pp. 22–5; and vol. 124, March 1936, pp. 24–8

'Prefabrication vocabulary: the panel-post construction', *California Arts and Architecture* (San Francisco), vol. 60, June 1943, pp. 32–3

'Notes . . . Modern Architecture' (unpublished manuscript), Los Angeles 1944

'Architect – postwar – post everybody', *Pencil Points* (New York), vol. 25, October 1944, pp. 16–18; and November 1944, pp. 12–14

'Discussion', *Pencil Points* (New York), vol. 25, November 1944, p. 16; and December 1944, p. 8

'Reference Frames in Space', *Architect and Engineer* (San Francisco), vol. 165, April 1946, pp. 10, 40, 44–5

'Postwar Automobiles', *Architect and Engineer* (San Francisco), vol. 168, February 1947, pp. 12–14

'Schindler Frame', *Architectural Record* (New York), vol. 101, May 1947, pp. 143–6

'Houses U.S.A.', letter to the editor, *Architectural Forum* (Boston), vol. 87, August 1947, p. 22

'A Great Debate' (on the United Nations Building), *Architectural Forum* (Boston), November 1950, p. 15

'Space Architecture', *Atelier* (Sydney, Australia), vol. 13, no. 1, November 1951, pp. 10–11

'Visual Technique' (unpublished manuscript), Los Angeles 1952

On R. M. Schindler

PATRICK ABERCROMBIE, *The Book of Modern Houses*, London 1936, pp. 298–9

WAYNE ANDREWS, *Architecture, Ambition and Americans*, New York 1955, pp. 274–5

J. B. BAKEMA, 'Schindler spel met de Ruimte', *Forum* (Amsterdam), vol. 16, no. 8, 1961, pp. 253–63

REYNER BANHAM, 'Rudolph Schindler – A Pioneer without Tears', *Architectural Design* (London), vol. 37, December 1967, pp. 578–9

—— *The Architecture of the Well-Tempered Environment*, London 1969, pp. 204–7

SHELDON CHENEY, *New World Architecture*, New York 1930, p. 288

DAVID GEBHARD, 'R.M. Schindler in New Mexico – 1915', *The New Mexico Architect* (Roswell, N.M.), vol. 7, January–February 1965, pp. 15–21
—— R.M. *Schindler – Architect*, catalogue of an exhibition at the Art Galleries, University of California, Santa Barbara, 1967
—— 'Ambiguity in the Work of R.M. Schindler', *Lotus* (Milan), no. 5, 1968, pp. 107–21

DAVID GEBHARD and ROBERT WINTER, *A Guide to Architecture in Southern California*, Los Angeles 1965, pp. 10–16

HERMAN HERTZBERGER, 'Dedicato a Schindler', *Domus* (Milan), no. 465, September 1967, pp. 2–7

LUDWIG HILBERSHEIMER, *International Neue Baukunst*, Stuttgart 1928, p. 9

HENRY-RUSSELL HITCHCOCK, 'An Eastern Critic Looks at Western Architecture', *California Arts and Architecture* (San Francisco), vol. 57, December 1940, pp. 21–3, 40

HANS HOLLEIN, 'Rudolph M. Schindler', *Der Aufbau* (Vienna), no. 3, 1961
—— 'Rudolph M. Schindler', *Bau* (Vienna), no. 4, 1966, pp. 67–82

ELAINE JANSON, 'Biographical Notes on R.M. Schindler Architect' (unpublished), *c.* 1938

ESTHER McCOY, 'West Coast Architecture: A Romantic Movement Ends', *Pacific Spectator* (Stanford, Calif.), vol. 7, no. 1, Winter 1953, pp. 20–30
—— 'Four Schindler Houses of the 1920s', *Arts and Architecture* (San Francisco), vol. 70, September 1953, pp. 12–14
—— 'R.M. Schindler', *Arts and Architecture* (San Francisco), vol. 71, May 1954, pp. 12–15
—— 'A Work by R.M. Schindler: Visual Expansion of a Small House', *Los Angeles Times* Sunday magazine section, 2 May 1954, pp. 14–15
—— 'Roots of California Contemporary Architecture', *Arts and Architecture* (San Francisco), vol. 73, October 1956, pp. 14–17
—— 'Letters of Louis H. Sullivan to R.M. Schindler', *Journal of the Society of Architectural Historians*, vol. 20, December 1961, pp. 179–84
—— 'R.M. Schindler 1887–1953', *Five California Architects*, New York 1960, pp. 149–93
—— 'The Growth of Cubism in the Work of R.M. Schindler', paper presented at the annual meeting of the Society of Architectural Historians, Los Angeles, January 1965 (unpublished)
—— 'Renewed Interest in Popularity of Schindler's Architecture', *Los Angeles Times* Calendar, 23 October 1967, p. 46
—— 'R.M. Schindler', *Lotus* (Milan), no. 5, 1968, pp. 92–105

CAREY McWILLIAMS, *Southern California Country*, New York 1946, pp. 354–62

RICHARD J. NEUTRA, *Wie Baut Amerika?*, Stuttgart 1927, pp. 53–7
—— *Amerika II*, Vienna 1930, pp. 128–32, 139

EDWIN PONDEXER, 'America's Own Architecture', *Building Age and National Builder* (New York), vol. 48, December 1936, p. 97

KAY SMALL, 'Hollywood Architects in International Contest', *Hollywood Magazine* (Hollywood), December 1928, p. 9

WALTER SEGAL, 'The Least Appreciated: Rudolph Schindler: 1887–1953', *The Architects Journal* (London), vol. 149, February 1969, pp. 476–9

BRUNO TAUT, *Modern Architecture*, London 1929, p. 98
—— *Die Neue Baukunst in Europa und Amerika*, Stuttgart 1929, pp. 178–9

BRUNO ZEVI, 'R. M. Schindler: Austria e California in una composizione diversa da Richard Neutra', *L'Architettura* (Milan), vol. 6, October 1960, pp. 422–3

'Unusual Home is Built of Concrete and Glass', *Popular Mechanics Magazine* (Chicago), vol. 48, June 1927, p. 969

Illustrations of buildings by Schindler

1912　*Der Architekt* (Vienna), vol. 29: Clubhouse for Actors, Vienna

1916　*Western Architecture* (Minneapolis and Chicago), vol. 24, November: works for Ottenheimer, Stern and Reichert

1917　*Western Architect* (Minneapolis and Chicago), vol. 25, April: project for Martin house, Taos
　　　Catalog, 13th Annual Chicago Architectural Club Exhibition: project for Martin house, Taos

1927　Bruno Taut, *Bauen* (Leipzig and Berlin), p. 56: Pueblo Ribera, La Jolla
　　　Bruno Taut, *Bauen der Neue Wohnbau* (Leipzig and Berlin), pp. 114–16: Pueblo Ribera, La Jolla
　　　'Unusual Home is Built of Concrete and Glass', *Popular Mechanics Magazine* (Chicago), vol. 48, June, p. 969: Lovell house, Newport Beach

1928　*Moderne Bauformen* (Stuttgart), vol. 28, pt 2, November, pp. 475–6: Packard house, Pasadena

1929　Bruno Taut, *Die neue Baukunst in Europa und Amerika* (Stuttgart), pp. 178–9: Howe house, Los Angeles
　　　Architectural Record (New York), vol. 65, January, pp. 5–9: Howe house, Los Angeles
　　　Architectural Record (New York), vol. 66, no. 3, September, pp. 257–61: Lovell house, Newport Beach

1930 *Modern Bauformen* (Stuttgart), vol. 6, June, p. 240: Lowes house, Eagle Rock
Architectural Record (New York), vol. 67, July, pp. 17–21: Pueblo Ribera, La Jolla
Western Architect (Minneapolis and Chicago), vol. 39, August, pls. 117, 118: Pueblo Ribera, La Jolla

1931 *Architectural Record* (New York), vol. 70, September, pp. 157 64: Wolfe house, Catalina Island

1932 *Creative Art* (New York), vol. 10, February, p. 112: Wolfe house, Catalina Island, and Elliot house, Los Angeles
T-Square (Philadelphia), vol. 2, February, pp. 20–21: Schindler-Chase house, Hollywood
Kokusai Kenchiku (Tokyo), vol. 8, April: Elliot house, Los Angeles

1933 *Architectural Review* (London), vol. 72, March, p. 117: Wolfe house, Catalina Island
Architectural Forum (Boston), vol. 58, pt 2, May, pp. 402–4: Sardi's Restaurant, Hollywood
Architectural Record (New York), vol. 74, August, p. 144: project for 'A Gasoline Station'

1934 Raymond McGrath, *Twentieth-Century Houses* (London), pp. 42, 112, 120: Wolfe house, Catalina Island
Architectural Forum (Boston), vol. 61, October, p. 231: Elliot house, Los Angeles

1935 *California Arts and Architecture* (San Francisco), vol. 47, January, p. 8, 18–19: Oliver house, Los Angeles; Wolfe house, Catalina Island
American Architect (Boston), vol. 146, May, pp. 23–6, 70–71: Oliver house, Los Angeles
Vomag (Pasadena), vol. 3, May, p. 17: Wolfe house, Catalina Island
Architect and Engineer (San Francisco), vol. 123, December, pp. 16–21, 26–7: Buck house, Los Angeles; Oliver house, Los Angeles; Wolfe house, Catalina Island

1936 *Kokusai Kenchiku* (Tokyo), vol. 12, March, pp. 56–7: Oliver house, Los Angeles
Clarté Art et art décoratif (Paris), vol. 9, February, cover and pp. 1–4: Oliver house, Los Angeles
Architectural Forum (Boston), vol. 65, pt 2, October, pp. 264–5: Buck house, Los Angeles

1937 *L'Architecture d'aujourd'hui* (Paris), vol. 8, no. 1, January, p. 63: Oliver house, Los Angeles
The Architect (London), February: McAlmon house, Los Angeles

The Architect and Building News (London), vol. 149, 19 February, pp. 240–41: Van Patten house, Los Angeles

Sunset (San Francisco), vol. 78, March, pp. 22–3: Oliver house, Los Angeles; Kaun house, Richmond

Architectural Record (New York), vol. 81, March, p. 89: Van Patten house, Los Angeles

Architectural Forum (Boston), vol. 66, April, pp. 340–41: McAlmon house, Los Angeles

California Arts and Architecture (San Francisco), vol. 51, May, p. 26: Kaun house, Richmond

Architectural Forum (Boston), vol. 67, July, pp. 31–2: Fitzpatrick house, Los Angeles

California Arts and Architecture (San Francisco), vol. 52, July, p. 28: McAlmon house, Los Angeles

Architectural Record (New York), vol. 82, September, pp. 87–8: Sunset Medical Buildings, Hollywood

The Architectural Forum, ed., *The 1938 Book of Small Houses* (New York), pp. 12–13: Kaun house, Richmond

1938   *Studio Yearbook of Decorative Art* (London): Buck house, Los Angeles; Fitzpatrick house, Los Angeles

      Architect and Engineer (San Francisco), vol. 134, August, p. 10: Rodakiewicz house, Los Angeles

      Kokusai Kenchiku (Tokyo), vol. 14, August: Van Patten house, Los Angeles

      Architectural Forum (Boston), vol. 69, November, pp. 362–3: Walker house, Los Angeles

      Nuestra Arquitectura (Buenos Aires), December, pp. 440–41: Walker house, Los Angeles

1940   James Ford and Katherine M. Ford, *The Modern House in America* (New York), pp. 101–3: McAlmon house, Los Angeles; Van Patten house, Los Angeles

      California Arts and Architecture (San Francisco), vol. 57, November, p. 26: Rodakiewicz house, Los Angeles

1941   *Los Angeles Times Home Magazine*, 16 March, p. 6: Rodakiewicz house, Los Angeles

      Pencil Points (New York), vol. 22, May, pp. 316–19, and October, p. 645: Rodakiewicz house, Los Angeles, and Pueblo Ribera, La Jolla

1942   *American Home* (New York), vol. 38, September, p. 48: Sachs apartments, Los Angeles

1943   *California Arts and Architecture* (San Francisco), vol. 60, January, pp. 32–3: Harris house, Los Angeles

1944   *Interiors* (New York), vol. 103, January, p. 41: Falk apartments, Los Angeles

      Arts and Architecture (San Francisco), vol. 61, February, pp. 21–3: Bennati cabin, Lake Arrowhead

American Home (Garden City, N.J.), vol. 31, April, pp. 18–19: Southall house, Los Angeles
Interiors (New York), vol. 103, August, p. 50: Pennington house, Thousand Oaks

1945   *Interiors* (New York), vol. 104, January, p. 82: Bethlehem Baptist Church, Los Angeles

1946   *California Plan Book* (San Francisco): Rodakiewicz house, Los Angeles; Van Dekker house, Canoga Park; Harris house, Los Angeles
The Californian (Los Angeles), vol. 1, May, pp. 58–9: Harris house, Los Angeles
Architects' Journal (London), vol. 104, 25 July, pp. 65–6: Bennati cabin, Lake Arrowhead
Interiors (New York), vol. 106, August, pp. 75–100: Bubeshko apartments, Los Angeles

1947   *California Plan Book* (San Francisco): Druckman house, Los Angeles
Architectural Forum (Boston), vol. 86, February, pp. 100–102: Van Dekker house, Canoga Park; Southall house, Los Angeles
Interiors (New York), vol. 107, August, p. 84: Falk apartments, Los Angeles
Sunset (San Francisco), vol. 99, December, p. 16: Presburger house, Studio City

1950   *Arts and Architecture* (San Francisco), vol. 67, January, pp. 36–7: Daugherty house, Encino
Perfect Home (Cedar Rapids, Iowa), March, pp. 8–9: Daugherty house, Encino
Arts and Architecture (San Francisco), vol. 67, April, p. 29: Lechner house, Studio City

1951   *Arts and Architecture* (San Francisco), vol. 68, November, p. 38: Toole house, Palm Village

Index